# Reading Comprehension

Teacher Created Materials

**Publisher:**
Rachelle Cracchiolo, M.S. Ed.

**Editor-in-Chief:**
Sharon Coan, M.S. Ed.

**Project Managers:**
Maria Elvira Gallardo, M.A.
Marcia Russell, M.A. Ed.

**Photo Credits:**
Corbis—pp. 5, 17, 21, 29, 45,
53, 57, 61, 65, 69, 81, 85, 93,
97, 101, 113, 121, 125
Photodisc—pp. 25
TCM—pp. 41, 105, 109
Art Explosion—pp. 9, 37, 89
Clipart.com—pp. 13, 33, 77
Ablestock—p. 129
Hemera—p. 117
Iztli Digital—p. 73

**Art Director:**
Lee Aucoin

**Designer:**
Lesley Palmer

**Product Developers:**
Teacher Created Materials
Creative Services, Inc.

**Product Manager:**
Phil Garcia

To order additional copies of this book or any other Teacher Created Materials products, go to www.tcmpub.com or call 1-800-858-7339.

**Teacher Created Materials**
5301 Oceanus Drive
Huntington Beach, CA 92649-1030
http://www.tcmpub.com
**ISBN 978-1-4258-0087-1**
©2006 Teacher Created Materials, Inc.
Reprinted 2013

# Table of Contents

# Introduction to Reading Comprehension

The lessons in this book will help you learn to understand what you read. Each lesson has a selection to read. Then you work with skills to help you understand what you read. Each lesson ends with a practice activity that helps you see what you know about the selection.

You can use these steps to help you as you work in the book. For each selection, follow these steps

**1.** Read the Before Reading questions.

### Before Reading
- Do you have brothers or sisters?
- How are you alike or different from your siblings?

**2.** Think about what you already know about the subject.

**3.** Read the selection. Use the During Reading questions.

### During Reading
- How did the brothers get along?
- How would you feel about moving?

**4.** Review the selection using the After Reading questions.

### After Reading
- Are there more than these kinds of bikes?
- Which kind of bike would you like to have?

**5.** Summarize and apply the information. Complete the activities in the book.

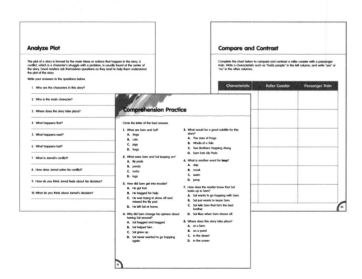

After completing all the activities, use the Comprehension Review section to review the information presented in the book. These pages also help you to check up on your skills.

# Up, Up, and Away!

| Before Reading | During Reading | After Reading |
|---|---|---|
| • What do you like to do with your grandparents?<br><br>• Have you ever flown a kite? | • Where did Dana get her kite?<br><br>• Why did Dana and her grandpa go to the park? | • Why did Dana say it was "the best day"?<br><br>• Do you think Grandpa had a great day? Why? |

Dana and her grandpa like to make things. Last week, Dana and her grandpa made a kite. It was a big kite! The kite had a lot of bright colors on it. Dana got white string to hold the kite. The kite even had a long, colorful tail. Dana and her grandpa spent a long time making the kite.

Today, Dana and her grandpa are at the park. They are going to fly the kite. First, Dana and her grandpa find a spot at the park. Next, Dana holds the kite. Then Grandpa lets out the string.

"Let go!" yells Grandpa. Dana lets the kite go. Up, up, up goes the kite.

"Wow!" cheers Dana. "Look at our kite fly! It is the best day!"

## Vocabulary

kite: a frame covered with paper that flies in the air

yell: to scream; to say something loudly

# Make Predictions

A prediction is a guess. A prediction is based on what you already know about a topic and what you have just learned about the same topic. Write your predictions for each event in the story "Up, Up, and Away!" Then write what really happened after reading the story.

|  | I Predict | Actually Happened |
|---|---|---|
| **1.** What did Dana and her grandpa make? |  |  |
| **2.** Why are Dana and her grandpa at the park? |  |  |
| **3.** What happened with the kite? |  |  |

#50087 Reading Comprehension—Level B

# Visualize

When you read a story, you can use the descriptions to create pictures in your mind, or visualize, what happened. The story "Up, Up, and Away!" tells about a girl and her grandpa who made a kite. Think about what the kite looked like. Draw a picture.

Write a sentence about your picture.

_____

_____

# Comprehension Practice

Circle the letter of the best answer.

1. What did Dana and her grandpa make?
   A. a plane
   B. a chest
   C. a kite
   D. laces

2. What color was the kite?
   A. all red
   B. yellow and blue
   C. lots of bright colors
   D. green and pink

3. Where did Dana and her grandpa go?
   A. a field
   B. the park
   C. a yard
   D. a playground

4. What did Dana cheer when the kite started to fly?
   A. Wow!
   B. Hooray!
   C. Yippee!
   D. Awesome!

5. What is this story mainly about?
   A. playing tag
   B. going for a walk
   C. flying a plane
   D. making a kite

6. When you **yell**, your voice is _____.
   A. soft
   B. loud
   C. a whisper
   D. low

7. What do you think Dana will do with the kite?
   A. lock it up in a box
   B. give it to someone else
   C. put it away and use it again
   D. throw it away

8. Which sentence from the story does NOT help the reader visualize the kite?
   A. The kite had a lot of bright colors on it.
   B. They are going to fly the kite.
   C. It was a big kite!
   D. The kite even had a long, colorful tail.

# Making a Snow Angel

### Before Reading

- How do you think you make a snow angel?

- What else is fun to do in the snow?

Snow falls in many places during the winter. Sometimes the snow is very wet and heavy. Sometimes the snow is fluffy and light like powder. When it is like powder, it is fun to make a snow angel.

Here is how you make a snow angel. First, find a clean spot of snow. Next, lie down on your back in the snow. Keep your arms and legs flat on the snow and then wave them up and down many times.

Last, stand up very carefully. Look at the ground. You will see your very own snow angel! Now you can give it a name and make more and more!

### During Reading

- What kind of snow is good for making snow angels?

- What is the second step in making a snow angel?

### After Reading

- Why does it matter if the snow is clean when you make a snow angel?

- If you made a snow angel, what would you name it?

### Vocabulary

fluffy: very light and soft

wave: to move back and forth or up and down

# Use Prior Knowledge and Make Connections

Think about "Making a Snow Angel." Write your answers to the following questions about the story.

1. What is the story about?

   _____

   _____

   _____

2. During which season does snow usually fall?

   _____

   _____

   _____

3. Describe two different kinds of snow.

   _____

   _____

   _____

4. Why should you stand up carefully after making a snow angel?

   _____

   _____

   _____

# Identify Sequence

Read "Making a Snow Angel." The story tells how to make a snow angel. It describes four steps. Put the steps in order from one to four. Then draw a picture of your own snow angel.

_____ Wave your hands and legs up and down against the ground.

_____ Find a clean spot of snow.

_____ Lie down on your back in the snow.

_____ Stand up very carefully and look at your snow angel.

**My Snow Angel**

# Comprehension Practice

Circle the letter of the best answer.

1. Where do you make a snow angel?
   A. on a hill
   B. in water
   C. on the ground
   D. on a table

2. What kind of snow is best for making a snow angel?
   A. fluffy
   B. melted
   C. frozen
   D. dirty

3. Snow falls mostly in _____.
   A. late June
   B. autumn
   C. early spring
   D. winter

4. How should you move your arms and legs when making a snow angel?
   A. up and down
   B. forward
   C. back and forth
   D. slowly

5. What is the main purpose of this story?
   A. to entertain with a funny story
   B. to warn about the dangers of snow
   C. to describe winter
   D. to show how to do something

6. What is **fluffy** snow like?
   A. hard
   B. wet
   C. soft
   D. fiery

7. During which month would you least likely be able to make a snow angel?
   A. June
   B. January
   C. February
   D. December

8. What is the last step in making a snow angel?
   A. Find clean snow.
   B. Stand up carefully.
   C. Wave arms back and forth.
   D. Lie down in the snow.

# Taking a Trip

## Before Reading
- Have you ever gone on a trip? Where?
- What kind of trip would you like to take? Why?

## During Reading
- What are three ways to travel?
- What sound do train tracks make?

## After Reading
- What do you think it feels like to be on a boat?
- How is a plane different from a boat?

It is fun to take a trip. You can travel by train, boat, or plane. A train trip is nice. You sit still, but the train is moving. You look out the window. The world passes by. The sound of the train goes clickety-clack. That is the sound of the train tracks.

A boat trip is fun. A boat takes you across water. You do not have to swim. You can stay dry. A boat goes up and down with the waves. Look at the water. Fish pass you by.

A plane trip is special. Planes fly high in the sky. You look out the window. Clouds pass by. You are higher than the birds. A plane trip can take you far away. Then it brings you home again.

A trip can be a fun adventure no matter how you go. A train, boat, or plane are all fun ways to see the world!

## Vocabulary

travel: to go from one place to another

train tracks: the metal rails trains run on

waves: when water goes up and down

# Classify/Categorize

Read "Taking a Trip." Think about the different ways to travel. Place the following details on the chart. Add your own detail to each category.

- takes you across water
- makes a clickety-clack sound
- takes you up in the air
- world passes by
- clouds pass by
- fish pass by

| Train Trip | Boat Trip | Plane Trip |
|---|---|---|
| | | |

# Fact and Opinion

A **fact** is something real. It can be proved. An **opinion** is what a person thinks or feels. Read each sentence below about "Taking a Trip." Circle "Fact" if it is true. Circle "Opinion" if it is how someone feels.

1. It is fun to take a trip.

   Fact              Opinion

2. A train trip is scary.

   Fact              Opinion

3. A boat takes you across water.

   Fact              Opinion

4. Planes fly high in the air.

   Fact              Opinion

5. A train rides on tracks.

   Fact              Opinion

6. A plane is better than a boat.

   Fact              Opinion

7. A plane has windows.

   Fact              Opinion

# Comprehension Practice

Circle the letter of the best answer.

1. Which of these is not mentioned in the story?
   A. train
   B. boat
   C. car
   D. plane

2. If you had to cross a lake, what would you take?
   A. a boat
   B. a train
   C. a bike
   D. a plane

3. What can you see outside a plane window?
   A. tracks
   B. clouds
   C. fish
   D. waves

4. What does the author say about boat trips?
   A. They are nice.
   B. They are special.
   C. They are scary.
   D. They are fun.

5. What does this story describe?
   A. different ways to travel
   B. how to fly a plane
   C. fun places to visit
   D. how to read a map

6. What does the word **across** mean?
   A. from one side to the other
   B. underneath
   C. high above
   D. right into

7. Which of these do you fly?
   A. car
   B. train
   C. plane
   D. boat

8. Which of the following is an opinion?
   A. A boat takes you across water.
   B. Planes go high up in the sky.
   C. Trains ride on tracks.
   D. I don't know why anybody would go on a train!

# The Cookout

It is summertime. The sun is out late. The air is warm. The summer breeze feels nice. Cindy invites her friends for a cookout. They will eat together outside.

Dad prepares fish. He adds oil and lemon. He places each fish on the grill. They will be ready in minutes. Mom adds fresh corn on the cob. Everything smells great! Cindy likes to help her parents at the grill.

Cindy's friends sit at a picnic table. Cindy gives each friend a plate. Dad serves the fish. Mom serves the corn. They place watermelon in the middle. Everyone wants a slice!

Mom has a good idea after dinner. "Let's play games," she says.

They decide to play tag. Cindy and her friends run around and around the picnic table. Mom and Dad play too.

It is still light outside when it is time to go. Cindy's friends agree. It is the best cookout ever!

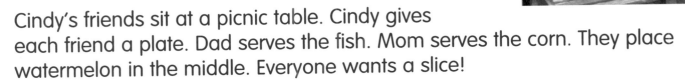

## Before Reading
- What foods do you like to eat in the summer?
- What foods are easy to eat outdoors?

## During Reading
- Why is summer a good time for a cookout?
- What game does Cindy play with her friends?

## After Reading
- How can you tell that Cindy's friends have fun at the cookout?
- What would you do with your friends at a cookout?

## Vocabulary

cookout: when you cook and eat food outside

breeze: a light wind

slice: a triangular piece cut from something, like a pie

# Analyze Plot Structure

Read "The Cookout." What does it tell about? Fill the chart with details from the story. Tell about the beginning, middle, and end.

**Beginning** _____

_____

_____

_____

**Middle** _____

_____

_____

_____

_____

_____

**End** _____

_____

_____

_____

_____

# Make Inferences

Answer these story questions and tell how you got your answer.

1. Does the weather spoil the cookout? How do you know?

_____

_____

_____

2. Do Cindy's friends like watermelon? How do you know?

_____

_____

_____

3. Has the sun set at the end of the story? How do you know?

_____

_____

_____

4. Do Cindy and her friends have a good time? How do you know?

_____

_____

_____

# Comprehension Practice

Circle the letter of the best answer.

1. Which character does not appear in this story?
   A. Mom
   B. Cindy
   C. Grandma
   D. Dad

2. What does everyone eat at the cookout?
   A. fish
   B. corn on the cob
   C. watermelon
   D. all of the above

3. How does Dad cook the fish?
   A. in a pan
   B. on the grill
   C. in a soup
   D. in the oven

4. What is Mom's good idea?
   A. She thinks they should go home.
   B. She thinks they should play games after dinner.
   C. She thinks they should have a cookout in the winter.
   D. She thinks they should go inside.

5. Where might you find this story?
   A. in a cookbook about ways to prepare fish dishes
   B. in a report titled "What I Did During Summer Vacation"
   C. in a book of fairytales
   D. in an encyclopedia under "Summer"

6. "Dad prepares fish." What does **prepare** mean?
   A. to buy
   B. to catch
   C. to get ready
   D. to eat

7. What does everyone do for fun at the end of the cookout?
   A. play tag
   B. go fishing
   C. eat watermelon
   D. wash all the dishes

8. Why is having a cookout fun?
   A. You can eat outside.
   B. Everyone can play games.
   C. The food is good.
   D. All of the above.

# Make Your Own Card

## Before Reading

- What kinds of cards have you received?
- When is a good time to send someone a card?

## During Reading

- What is the first step in making a card?
- What is the last step in making a card?

## After Reading

- Why should you think about who will get the card?
- Why is a card that you make one-of-a-kind?

Have you ever made your own card? It is fun. First, you need a sheet of paper. You can use red paper. You can use green, yellow, or violet paper. Choose a color you like best. Next, fold the paper in half. Fold it in half again. You have made a card!

Most cards have a message. Think about the person you will send the card to. What would you like to tell that person? Some cards say "Happy Birthday." Some say "Thank You" or "Get Well Soon." You can also make someone a card for a special holiday, like Valentine's Day, Mother's Day, or Father's Day. It's nice to write a note inside saying something special.

The last step is to decorate the card. Use markers to draw a picture on the front. Paste yarn to make a border around the note. You can add whatever you want. Your card will be special because it is a one-of-a-kind card made by you!

## Vocabulary

violet: a shade of purple

message: a short note

border: a frame around words or a drawing

# Use Prior Knowledge and Make Connections

Read "Make Your Own Card." Tell what you know about cards. Answer the following questions.

**1.** What do cards look like?

_____

_____

_____

**2.** What kinds of cards do people send?

_____

_____

_____

**3.** How does it feel to get a card?

_____

_____

_____

**4.** How is a card that you make different than a card from the store?

_____

_____

_____

# Identify Sequence

"Make Your Own Card" tells how to make a card step-by-step. Read the sentences below. Number the steps to show the right order. Reread the steps to check your answers. Draw a picture of a card you would like to make in the picture box.

_____ Write a message.

_____ Get a sheet of paper.

_____ Think about the person you will send the card to.

_____ Fold the paper in half. Fold it again.

_____ Draw a picture on the front.

# Comprehension Practice

Circle the letter of the best answer.

1. "Make Your Own Card" is _____.
   - A. a journal entry
   - B. a funny story
   - C. an instructional story
   - D. a newspaper article

2. Which sentence from the story tells an opinion?
   - A. It is fun.
   - B. Most cards have a message.
   - C. Some cards say "Happy Birthday."
   - D. Write a note inside.

3. Why should you think about who will get the card?
   - A. so they can help you decorate
   - B. to wish them a happy birthday
   - C. to borrow their markers
   - D. to decide what to tell them in a message

4. What is the last step in making a card?
   - A. choose the color of paper you like best
   - B. fold the paper in half
   - C. decorate the card
   - D. write a message

5. What is this story mainly about?
   - A. why you should make a card
   - B. when you should make a card
   - C. how you can make a card
   - D. where you can make a card

6. What does it mean to **decorate** a card?
   - A. to send it off
   - B. to put a stamp on it
   - C. to think about the person it is for
   - D. to make it look pretty

7. Which of the following is something you would NOT put in a card?
   - A. a get well wish
   - B. the date
   - C. a picture
   - D. a cupcake

8. What is the first thing you need to make a card?
   - A. a sheet of paper
   - B. a message
   - C. yarn
   - D. markers

# At the Library

Have you been to a library lately? A library has all the books you need. It has books that tell your favorite stories. It has books on any topic you can name. It does not cost money to borrow a book. All you need is a library card. You can get a card at the front desk. The card will have your name on it.

Libraries today have more than just books. Some have movies. Some have music. You can borrow movies or music with your card too.

Most libraries have a place just for kids. This is the best part of the library. Everything you want is in one place. You can ask a librarian for help. A librarian knows where everything belongs. Librarians can help you find what you need.

So find your local library and hit the books today!

## Before Reading

- What do you do at the library?
- What kinds of books do you enjoy reading?

## During Reading

- Name some things you can find at the library.
- What kinds of questions can you ask a librarian?

## After Reading

- When is a good time to go to the library?
- Why is the library an important place?

## Vocabulary

topic: a subject of interest

borrow: to take something for awhile

librarian: someone who works in a library

local: in your neighborhood

# Classify/Categorize

Read "At the Library." Think about things that belong in a library. Read the list below. Separate the things that you can find at a library from the things you can't find at a library in the chart below.

| | | | | |
|---|---|---|---|---|
| books | clothes | movies | music | art supplies |
| televisions | a librarian | sports equipment | a front desk | |

| Found at the library | Not found at the library |
|---|---|
| | |

# Develop Vocabulary

The words below are from "At the Library." Read the article to learn what each word means. Write the definition next to the word. Then write a sentence using each new word.

**topic** _____

_____

_____

_____

**borrow** _____

_____

_____

_____

**librarian** _____

_____

_____

_____

# Comprehension Practice

Circle the letter of the best answer.

1. What does it cost to borrow a library book?
   A. nothing
   B. fifty cents
   C. two dollars
   D. three dollars

2. What do you need to get a book at the library?
   A. a book to trade
   B. an adult
   C. fifty cents
   D. a library card

3. Who can help you best in a library?
   A. a police officer
   B. a librarian
   C. your teacher
   D. a friend

4. Why might you go to a library?
   A. to talk to your friends
   B. to borrow art supplies
   C. to get a fun book to read
   D. to bother the librarian

5. This story is mainly about _____.
   A. things that can be found at a library
   B. how books are made
   C. ways to help your local library
   D. how to become a librarian

6. Which of the following means a subject that you like to read about?
   A. borrow
   B. topic
   C. movie
   D. book

7. What is one way to find a book about superheroes at the library?
   A. Look at all the movies on superheroes.
   B. Find the section on animals.
   C. Ask the librarian for help.
   D. Yell to others in the library for help.

8. What should you do just before you leave the library?
   A. Say bye to everyone.
   B. Put your books in a pile on the floor.
   C. Leave all of the books at the library.
   D. Check out the materials you want to borrow.

# Pizza Night

### Before Reading

- Have you ever made pizza?
- What toppings do you like to eat on your pizza?

### During Reading

- What do Gina's Mom and Dad do to prepare the pizza?
- What toppings does Gina put on her share of the pizza?

### After Reading

- Do you think Gina's family likes to spend time together?
- Does it matter in what order things are done to make a pizza? Why?

### Vocabulary

crust: a hard outer surface of some foods

pile: to stack in a heap

pizza: a baked food with a crust, cheese, and other toppings

Gina was happy. It was Friday. Her family was making their own pizza for dinner. They did this every week.

Dad made the pizza crust and put the pizza sauce on top. Mom got all the toppings ready. She put them in bowls. Then everyone put their favorite toppings on their share of the pizza crust.

Gina's little sister Anna only likes cheese. "More! More!" she yelled as she piled it on.

"I will have sauce, cheese, pepperoni, and onions," Gina said. Mom and Dad like the same things. Their share of the pizza had sauce, cheese, sausage, mushrooms, black olives, and green peppers. Then Mom put the pizza in the oven for 20 minutes.

The pizza was very colorful. They ate the pizza together. It was delicious! Gina wished every day was pizza night!

# Identify Sequence

"Pizza Night" tells how Gina's family makes their own pizza. List the steps of the process in order below.

| Steps to Make a Pizza | |
|---|---|
| 1. | |
| 2. | |
| 3. | |
| 4. | |
| 5. | |

# Visualize

Think about the pizza that Gina's family made in "Pizza Night." Make a picture in your mind of what the pizza looked like. Draw the picture you see in your mind. Check the details in the story.

**Family Friday Pizza**

Tell how the picture of the pizza helps you understand the story better.

_____

_____

# Comprehension Practice

Circle the letter of the best answer.

1. Why is Friday special for Gina?
   A. Her school has Pizza Night.
   B. She goes to the park.
   C. She makes pizza with her family.
   D. It is her birthday.

2. How many things does Anna like on her pizza?
   A. five
   B. one
   C. three
   D. four

3. What does Gina say about Mom and Dad?
   A. They like to ride bikes.
   B. They go to work.
   C. They are very nice.
   D. They like the same things.

4. What does Gina wish?
   A. that Tuesday was pizza night
   B. that she had her own pizza
   C. that they would make pizza every day
   D. that her sister behaved better

5. According to the story, Gina and her family _____ .
   A. go out for dinner on Fridays
   B. make pizza for dinner every week
   C. all like onions on their pizza
   D. do not enjoy eating pizza

6. If cheese is your **favorite** topping, what does that mean?
   A. that you can't like any other toppings
   B. that it is your best friend
   C. that you do not like the way it tastes
   D. that it is the topping you like the best

7. What is the first step in making a pizza?
   A. stir the pizza sauce
   B. take it out of the oven
   C. make the pizza crust
   D. put on the cheese

8. Which sentence in the story helps you visualize the pizza?
   A. Mom got all the toppings ready.
   B. Her family was making their own pizza for dinner.
   C. Gina's little sister Anna only likes cheese.
   D. Their share of the pizza had sauce, cheese, sausage, mushrooms, black olives, and green peppers.

# Pen Pals

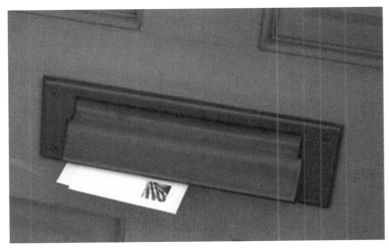

Have you ever had a pen pal? A pen pal is someone you talk with through letters. You use a pen and paper to share ideas. You may never meet your pen pal. You may not know what your pen pal looks like. Imagine walking by a kid on the street. It could be your pen pal and you might not even know it!

Pen pals can live nearby. Some live in another country. A pen pal from far away is fun. You can tell your pen pal all about your home and your family. They will write about their home and family. You can discover a new place. In some ways, the place will be different. In many ways, it will be the same.

The best part about a pen pal is that you get lots of mail. Keep writing letters to your pen pal. Then look in the mailbox. One of those envelopes might just be for you!

## Before Reading
- Would you like to have a pen pal? Why or why not?
- What stories would you share with your pen pal?

## During Reading
- What could happen if you never see your pen pal?
- What can pen pals from far away tell you about?

## After Reading
- What must you do to keep a pen pal?
- Why might there be an envelope for you in the mailbox?

## Vocabulary

pen pal: a person you write to and get letters from

discover: to learn something new

envelopes: a paper pocket for letters

# Develop Vocabulary

The words below are from "Pen Pals." Read the article to learn what each word means. Write the definition next to the word. Then write a sentence using each new word.

**pen pal** _____

_____

_____

_____

**discover** _____

_____

_____

_____

**envelopes** _____

_____

_____

_____

# Fact and Opinion

A **fact** is something real. It can be proven. An **opinion** is what a person thinks or feels. Read each sentence below about the article "Pen Pals." Circle "Fact" if it is true. Circle "Opinion" if it is how someone feels.

1.  A pen pal is someone you talk with through letters.

    Fact            Opinion

2.  Pen pals can live nearby.

    Fact            Opinion

3.  A pen pal from far away is fun.

    Fact            Opinion

4.  The best part about a pen pal is that you get lots of mail.

    Fact            Opinion

5.  It is important to know what your pen pal looks like.

    Fact            Opinion

6.  Letters from your pen pal are put in your mailbox.

    Fact            Opinion

7.  You should never tell your pen pal about your family.

    Fact            Opinion

# Comprehension Practice

Circle the letter of the best answer.

1. What is this story mainly about?
   A. sharing ideas
   B. discovering new places
   C. having a pen pal
   D. telling about your family

2. What two things do you need to share ideas with a pen pal?
   A. a ball and a glove
   B. a paintbrush and paints
   C. a telephone for each pal
   D. a pen and paper

3. What does the author suggest you tell a pen pal about?
   A. what you look like
   B. why you like animals
   C. your home and family
   D. what you had for dinner

4. What is the author's favorite part about having a pen pal?
   A. getting lots of mail
   B. discovering a new place
   C. not knowing what the pal looks like
   D. learning how places are the same

5. Which is NOT true about the main topic of this story?
   A. A pen pal can live in another country.
   B. A pen pal mails you letters.
   C. A pen pal always works in a library.
   D. You can discover a new place through a pen pal.

6. What does the word **discover** mean in the story?
   A. to write to a new friend
   B. to learn something you did not know
   C. to travel to a foreign country
   D. to use a new invention

7. Which of the following is true about a pen pal?
   A. A pen pal is someone you communicate with through letters.
   B. A pen pal does not know how to write yet.
   C. A pen pal is always talking.
   D. A pen pal is someone you know everything about.

8. Which of the following is an opinion?
   A. My pen pal is coming to visit me.
   B. I write to my pen pal each week.
   C. I received a letter on Friday.
   D. My pen pal has nice handwriting.

# In the Garden

Gardens come in all shapes and sizes. Some gardens grow rows of vegetables in the soil. They grow things like peas, corn, and beans. Ripe food from the garden tastes great.

Other gardens grow flowers. There are many kinds of flowers. No two gardens ever look the same. Flower gardens are good for smelling.

Spring is the best time to be in a garden. There is plenty of sun and water in spring. Plants need these things to grow. Bugs come to life in a spring garden. Bees buzz. Ladybugs fly. Worms wiggle. Butterflies flutter. A garden is full of living things.

I have a small herb garden. It grows right inside my house! I grow herbs like mint and bay leaves on my window sill. My indoor garden makes it fun to cook. You should try it sometime!

## Before Reading

- Why might someone like to have a garden?
- What would you plant in a garden?

## During Reading

- What are two things a plant needs to grow?
- What are some foods you can find in a vegetable garden?

## After Reading

- Why is spring a nice time to be in a garden?
- What are the three kinds of gardens in this story?

## Vocabulary

ripe: ready to eat

flutter: to wave back and forth

herbs: plants used in cooking for flavor

# Classify/Categorize

Read "In the Garden." Then read the list below. Decide which things you would find in a garden. Place each item where it belongs in the chart.

| | | | | | |
|---|---|---|---|---|---|
| bees | clouds | ladybugs | clothes | bread | flowers |
| soil | sunflowers | books | corn | weeds | worms |

| Found in a Garden | Not Found in a Garden |
|---|---|
| | |

# Compare and Contrast

"In the Garden" tells about different kinds of gardens. Think about flower gardens and vegetable gardens. How are they alike? How are they different? Complete the chart with details from the article. Add details of your own.

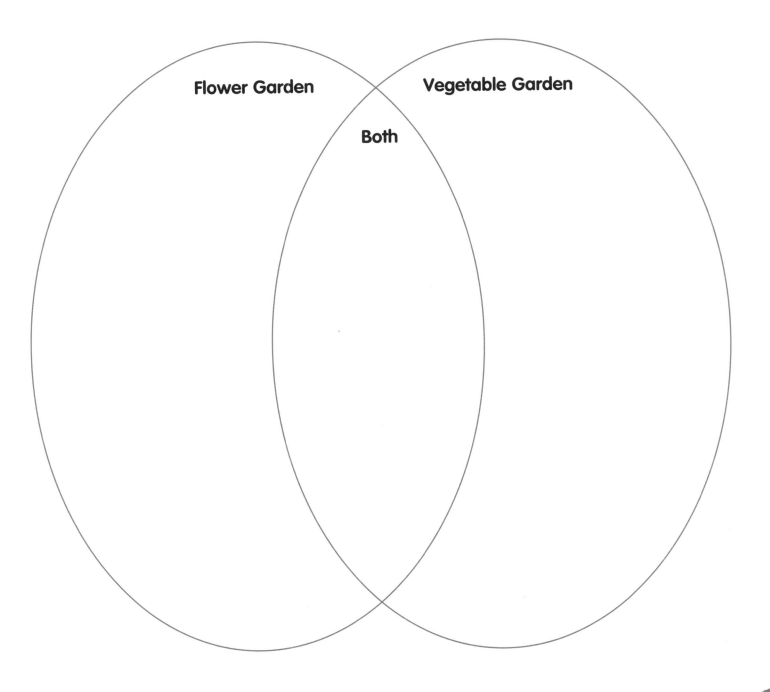

**Flower Garden**

**Both**

**Vegetable Garden**

# Comprehension Practice

Circle the letter of the best answer.

1. What are two things plants need to grow?
   A. rice and heat
   B. sand and waves
   C. milk and cookies
   D. sun and water

2. What is the best thing to do with garden vegetables?
   A. eat them with dinner
   B. use them to make art
   C. place them under your pillow for luck
   D. hide them around your home

3. Which statement below appears in the story?
   A. A garden is full of living things.
   B. Ladybugs wiggle.
   C. Moonlight is good for plants.
   D. A garden is a nice place to take a nap.

4. Where is the author's herb garden?
   A. in the backyard
   B. on a window sill
   C. at the park
   D. in front of the house

5. What is this story mainly about?
   A. kinds of gardens
   B. springtime
   C. pretty flowers
   D. cooking with herbs

6. Which of the following **flutters**?
   A. a ladybug's leg
   B. a butterfly's wings
   C. a bee's buzzer
   D. a worm's body

7. Which of these are herbs?
   A. rose leaves
   B. pumpkins
   C. apples
   D. mint

8. How are vegetable gardens similar to herb gardens?
   A. Vegetable gardens grow lots of flowers.
   B. Vegetable gardens grow inside the house.
   C. Vegetable gardens produce things that can be eaten.
   D. Bay leaves and mint grow in vegetable gardens.

# The Haircut

Mom said it was time for Josh to get a haircut. So she took him to the barbershop after school. Josh loved getting his hair cut. He had known his barber as long as he could remember.

"I want the same haircut as my dad," Josh tells the barber. "I think I can do that," says the barber.

The barber uses the buzz clippers to shave hair from the bottom of Josh's neck. Then he uses scissors. He cuts a little hair from the top. He trims carefully around the ears. He shortens the hair in front. Snip, snip, snip. When he is done, he shows Josh a mirror.

"How do you like it?" the barber asks.

Josh looks at his hair in the mirror. "I like it," he says. "I look just like Dad."

The barber smiles. "Yes, you do," he says. He should know. He is Josh's dad.

## Before Reading
- Why is it important to get a haircut regularly?
- Who cuts your hair?

## During Reading
- How long has Josh known his barber?
- What does the barber use to shave the hair at the bottom of Josh's neck?

## After Reading
- What words tell you Josh likes his haircut?
- What is surprising about the story's ending?

## Vocabulary
barber: a person who cuts hair

buzz clippers: electric blades that can cut hair short

trims: cuts a small amount

# Make Predictions

Think about what will happen as you read "The Haircut," and write your predictions in the chart below.

| | | |
|---|---|---|
| **1.** | Where will Mom take Josh to get a haircut? | |
| **2.** | Who will cut Josh's hair? | |
| **3.** | How will the barber cut Josh's hair? | |
| **4.** | Will Josh like his haircut? | |
| **5.** | Will his haircut look like Dad's? | |
| **6.** | Where will Josh go to get haircuts in the future? | |

# Analyze Plot Structure

"The Haircut" tells a story from start to finish. Fill in the chart with details from the story. Tell about the beginning, middle, and end.

**Beginning**

**Main Idea:** Mom takes Josh to the barber shop.

**Details:** _____

_____

_____

**Middle**

**Main Idea:** The barber cuts Josh's hair.

**Details:** _____

_____

_____

**End**

**Main Idea:** Josh looks at his haircut in the mirror.

**Details:** _____

_____

_____

# Comprehension Practice

Circle the letter of the best answer.

1. What reason best explains why Josh need a haircut?
   A. He is going to a party.
   B. Josh's hair is getting long.
   C. The barber shop is his dad's.
   D. The weather is hot.

2. What object does the barber hand to Josh?
   A. a mirror
   B. the buzz clippers
   C. hair gel
   D. scissors

3. What does the barber do first?
   A. He trims the hair around Josh's ears.
   B. He cuts hair from the top of Josh's head.
   C. He shortens Josh's hair in front.
   D. He shaves the hair from the back of Josh's neck.

4. Why does Josh like his haircut?
   A. He does not like long hair.
   B. His haircut looks like his dad's haircut.
   C. His haircut makes him look older.
   D. Now he won't have as much hair to wash.

5. What is this story about?
   A. barber school
   B. Josh and his mother
   C. Josh's haircut
   D. a joke on Josh

6. What is the meaning of **trim**?
   A. to make hair longer
   B. to cut your own hair
   C. to only cut a little bit of hair
   D. to shave the hair on your face

7. Why do you think Josh got a haircut?
   A. His mom said that he needed one.
   B. Some kids laughed at his long hair.
   C. His hair was not dark enough.
   D. He didn't want to comb his hair anymore.

8. What does the reader discover at the end of the story?
   A. Josh is going to star in a movie.
   B. The barber is actually Josh's dad.
   C. Josh's uncle is also a barber.
   D. Josh did not really need a haircut.

# Lunch Time

It is time for lunch. What are your favorite foods? I like peanut butter and jelly sandwiches. They taste great. And they are so easy to make. Do you know how to make a sandwich? It is as easy as one, two, three.

You do not need a stove or oven for this recipe. First, you take two pieces of bread. Place them on a plate. Next, spread a little peanut butter on one slice. If you really like peanut butter, spread a thick layer. Now it is jelly time. What flavor of jelly do you like best? I like grape. It is the tastiest. Spread jelly on the other slice of bread. Your sandwich is almost complete.

The last step is to join the two slices of bread together. Leave it whole or cut it in half. Finally, get a napkin and your favorite drink. Enjoy!

## Before Reading

- What are your favorite lunch time foods?
- What foods do you know how to make yourself?

## During Reading

- Why don't you need an oven or stove for this recipe?
- What should you do if you like peanut butter a lot?

## After Reading

- What ingredients does this recipe call for?
- Do you need to use grape jelly to make this sandwich?

## Vocabulary

recipe: a set of directions for making food

spread: to apply a layer on top of something

join: combine together

# Fact and Opinion

Read "Lunch Time." This article tells both facts and opinions. A **fact** is something real. It can be proven. An **opinion** is what a person thinks or feels. Read each sentence below about the article. Circle "Fact" if it is true. Circle "Opinion" if it is how someone feels.

1.  The author likes peanut butter and jelly sandwiches.

    Fact            Opinion

2.  Peanut butter and jelly sandwiches taste great.

    Fact            Opinion

3.  You do not need a stove or oven for this recipe.

    Fact            Opinion

4.  Grape is the tastiest jelly.

    Fact            Opinion

5.  You need to spread the peanut butter on the bread.

    Fact            Opinion

# Identify Sequence

"Lunch Time" tells how to make something step by step. Read the sentences below. Number the steps to show the right order from one to five. Reread the steps to check your answers.

_____ Spread jelly on the other slice of bread.

_____ Place two pieces of bread on a plate.

_____ Join the two slices of bread together.

_____ Enjoy!

_____ Spread peanut butter on one slice of bread.

Draw a picture of the things you need to make a peanut butter and jelly sandwich.

# Comprehension Practice

Circle the letter of the best answer.

1. What is this story mainly about?
   A. different kinds of sandwiches
   B. when to make a sandwich
   C. how to make a sandwich
   D. the best jelly to use in a sandwich

2. Which sentence from the story asks a question?
   A. It is time for lunch.
   B. What flavor of jelly do you like best?
   C. Your sandwich is almost complete.
   D. Enjoy!

3. What is the author's favorite kind of jelly?
   A. grape
   B. strawberry
   C. orange
   D. all of the above

4. What is the last step in making the sandwich?
   A. join the two slices of bread together
   B. spread a thick layer of peanut butter
   C. take two pieces of bread
   D. spread jelly on the other slice of bread

5. What is another good title for this story?
   A. Lunch Party
   B. Eating Out
   C. Let's Make a Sandwich
   D. Bread is Better

6. When you **spread** peanut butter on bread, what do you do?
   A. spray it all over the bread
   B. roll it up with the bread
   C. bake it into the bread
   D. put a layer of it on the bread

7. Which of the following from the story is a fact?
   A. They taste great.
   B. I like grape. It is the tastiest.
   C. You do not need a stove or oven for this recipe.
   D. And they are so easy to make.

8. When do you spread the jelly?
   A. after you join the two slices of bread together
   B. after you take the bread from the stove
   C. after you spread peanut butter on one slice
   D. before you lay the bread on the plate

# Surprise Friends

## Before Reading

- Do you have a pet?
- Do you have a best friend?

Many people have dogs as pets. Many people have cats as pets. Some people don't have both dogs and cats as pets. They think they might not get along.

Bucky is a dog. Smokey is a cat. Bucky and Smokey are best friends. They chase each other. They nibble on each other. They sleep next to each other.

Sometimes Bucky and Smokey play hide-and-seek. Smokey hides. Bucky sniffs and tries to find Smokey. When he finds him, Bucky the dog chases Smokey the cat. Smokey runs fast.

They get tired from playing. They drink lots of water, cuddle, and take a nap. When they have rested, they play again. Bucky the dog and Smokey the cat are best friends. Isn't that a surprise?

## During Reading

- How are Smokey and Bucky different?
- What is one thing Smokey and Bucky do together?

## After Reading

- What do Smokey and Bucky do when they get tired from playing?
- Do you do the things Smokey and Bucky do with your best friend?

## Vocabulary

nibble: to bite gently and playfully

cuddle: to lie closely next to someone or something

sniff: to smell for something

# Use Prior Knowledge and Make Connections

Think about "Surprise Friends." Think about what you already knew about dogs and cats.

Did you learn something new? What?

_____

_____

Draw a picture that shows something surprising about dogs and cats. Give your picture a title.

_____

# Make Predictions

Read "Surprise Friends." Answer the questions by telling what comes next.

1. What happens when Bucky chases Smokey?

   _____

   _____

2. What does Bucky do when Smokey hides?

   _____

   _____

3. After they run around and play chase, what will they do?

   _____

   _____

4. When Bucky and Smokey are rested, what will they do again?

   _____

   _____

# Comprehension Practice

Circle the letter of the best answer.

1. What is a surprise about Bucky and Smokey?
   A. They like snow.
   B. They get along.
   C. They swim.
   D. They fight.

2. How do they sleep?
   A. in a bed
   B. on a rug
   C. side by side
   D. under a blanket

3. What do they drink?
   A. water
   B. milk
   C. coffee
   D. orange juice

4. What does Bucky do to find Smokey when he hides?
   A. barks his name
   B. shuts his eyes
   C. cries
   D. sniffs

5. The second paragraph is mainly about _____.
   A. why Bucky and Smokey don't get along
   B. what Bucky and Smokey eat
   C. how Bucky and Smokey play
   D. how dogs make good pets

6. What is the meaning of **nibble**?
   A. to bite softly
   B. to cuddle
   C. to sniff
   D. to hurt

7. What does Bucky like to do?
   A. chase Smokey
   B. sniff and try to find Smokey
   C. play hide-and-seek
   D. all of the above

8. What can we predict about Bucky and Smokey?
   A. They will not get along in the future.
   B. Bucky will stop playing with Smokey.
   C. Smokey will run away with another cat.
   D. They will be friends forever.

# Music Makers

### Before Reading

- What kind of music do you like best?
- What kind of instrument would you like to play?

### During Reading

- How is a banjo played?
- What instrument does Carmen's brother play?

### After Reading

- What is Carmen's favorite dream?
- What do Carmen and David do at the end when their favorite song is on the radio?

Carmen loves music. She plays the banjo. She plucks the strings to play the songs she likes best. Pluck, pluck, pluck. She can play all day long. At night she dreams of playing on stage. The lights shine on her as she plays her banjo. All her friends come to see. It is her favorite dream.

Her younger brother, David, likes music too. He plays the drums with his sticks. He makes rat-a-tat sounds. Rat-a-tat thump. He and Carmen play together. They sound great. Maybe they will start a band one day.

David has an idea. "Turn on the radio, Carmen. It is our favorite tune! We can play along." Carmen gets her banjo. David plays his drums. Pluck, pluck, pluck. Rat-a-tat thump. What a couple of music makers!

### Vocabulary

banjo: a small musical instrument with strings

stage: an area set apart for performers

tune: another word for a song

# Compare and Contrast

Read "Music Makers." Carmen and her younger brother, David, both make music, but they play different instruments. Compare and contrast the banjo and the drums below. How are they alike? How are they different?

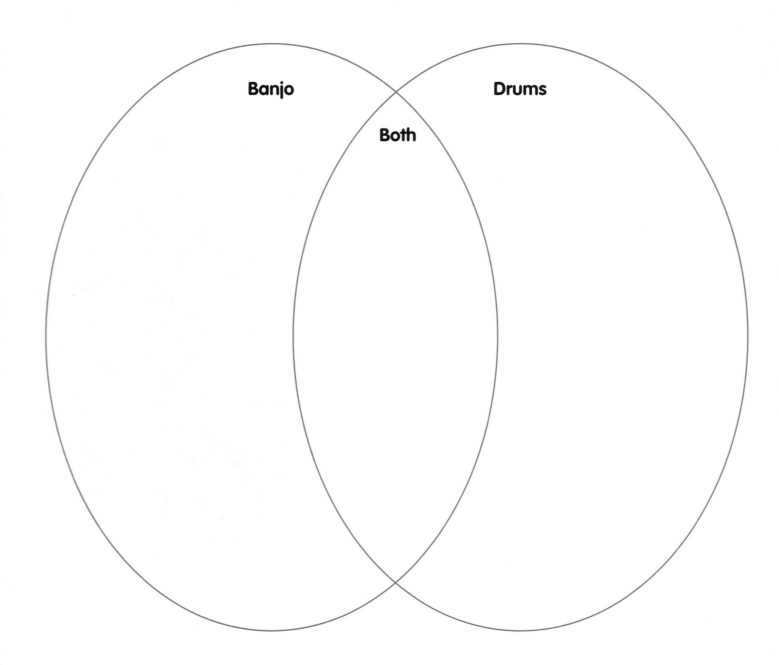

**Banjo**

**Drums**

**Both**

# Visualize

Carmen has a special dream. She dreams about playing the banjo on stage. Reread the story and picture all of the details.

Draw a picture to show Carmen's dream. Make a title for your picture. Write two sentences about your picture.

_____

_____
_____
_____
_____

# Comprehension Practice

Circle the letter of the best answer.

1. Why does Carmen play the banjo?
   A. She is bored.
   B. She likes music.
   C. She cannot play the drums.
   D. She does not have friends.

2. What does Carmen do in her favorite dream?
   A. makes a banjo
   B. plays music on stage
   C. gets a radio
   D. plays the drums

3. What sound do the drums make?
   A. rat-a-tat thump
   B. clang, clang, clang
   C. pluck, pluck, pluck
   D. jingle jangle jingle

4. Carmen and her brother will probably _____.
   A. join a sports team
   B. stop making music
   C. sell their radio
   D. start a band one day

5. What is the main topic of this story?
   A. ways to become a professional musician
   B. Carmen and David's love of music
   C. how much Carmen's brother bothers her
   D. starting your own music group

6. What is another word for **song**?
   A. pluck
   B. whistle
   C. tune
   D. drum

7. How is a banjo different from the drums?
   A. It has a pedal.
   B. It has strings.
   C. It has sticks.
   D. It goes rat-a-tat.

8. Which sentence helps the reader visualize Carmen on stage?
   A. He plays the drums with his sticks.
   B. The lights shine on her as she plays her banjo.
   C. David has an idea.
   D. Carmen loves music.

# Art Museums

An art museum is a fun place to be. You can see all kinds of art. Go see the paintings on display. Some are big and some are small. Some are all one color and some show many colors. There are so many exciting ways to paint. No two paintings are ever the same. Artists make each artwork an original piece.

Go see the sculptures. There are sculptures made of clay. There are sculptures made of wood. Sculptures can be made from anything, even metal or objects you find on the ground. You can walk all the way around a sculpture. I like to look at sculptures from the back.

Some art museums have a corner just for kids. You can learn about art history in these places. Sometimes you can create an artwork of your own. Be sure to practice at home to improve your skills. Maybe your art will be in a museum one day.

## Before Reading

- Have you ever been to an art museum?
- What artwork have you made in class?

## During Reading

- Can a painting show only one color?
- What objects can you use to make a sculpture?

## After Reading

- What can you do at an art museum?
- Why are no two artworks ever the same?

## Vocabulary

art museum: a place to look at art

original: one-of-a-kind

sculptures: three-dimensional artwork

# Identify Main Idea and Supporting Details

Read "Art Museums." The title helps you know what this article is mainly about. Fill in the missing blank in the center circle below. Then write down ideas that support the main idea. Write one detail in each circle about the main idea.

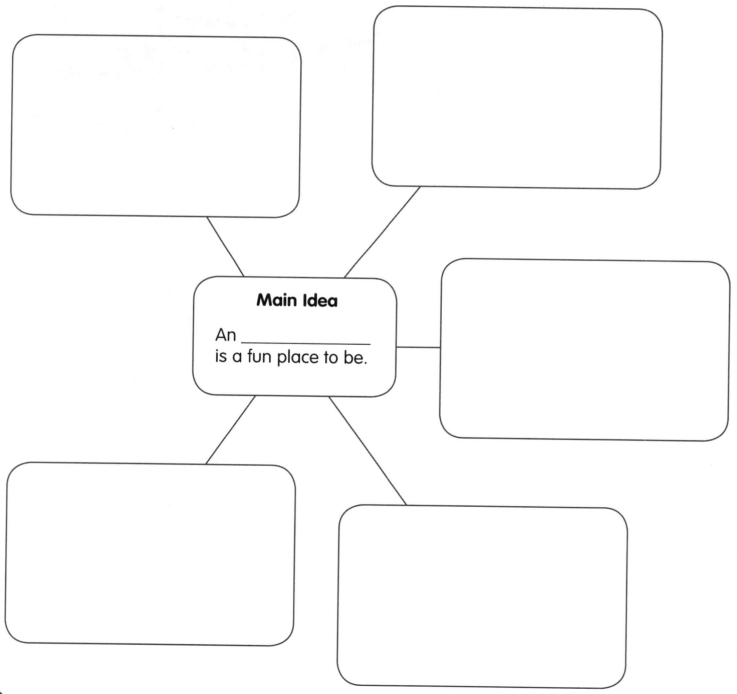

**Main Idea**

An _____ is a fun place to be.

© Teacher Created Materials

# Fact and Opinion

A **fact** is something real. It can be proven. An **opinion** is what a person thinks or feels. Read each sentence below about "Art Museums." Circle "Fact" if it is true. Circle "Opinion" if it is how someone feels.

**1.** An art museum is a fun place to be.

Fact                    Opinion

**2.** There are so many different ways to paint.

Fact                    Opinion

**3.** Artists make each artwork an original.

Fact                    Opinion

**4.** Sculptures are nicer than paintings.

Fact                    Opinion

**5.** You could see sculptures from the back.

Fact                    Opinion

**6.** Paintings come in many sizes.

Fact                    Opinion

**7.** Only adults really like museums.

Fact                    Opinion

# Comprehension Practice

Circle the letter of the best answer.

1. Which is the author's opinion about art museums?
   A. They are big.
   B. They are boring.
   C. They are just for kids.
   D. They are fun.

2. What kind of sculpture is not mentioned in the article?
   A. clay
   B. wood
   C. cloth
   D. metal

3. Why are no two paintings ever the same?
   A. They show many colors.
   B. Artists make each one an original.
   C. You can walk all the way around them.
   D. Some are small.

4. Why does the author suggest you practice making artwork at home?
   A. to improve
   B. to see all kinds of art
   C. to learn about art history
   D. to use objects you find on the ground

5. What is the message of this selection?
   A. Art museums are not worth visiting.
   B. Art museums are hard to find.
   C. There are good restaurants at museums.
   D. There are many interesting things to see at art museums.

6. What does **one-of-a kind** mean?
   A. ordinary
   B. the same
   C. unique
   D. more than one

7. Which is NOT found in an art museum?
   A. sketches
   B. sculptures
   C. rock bands
   D. paintings

8. Which is NOT true?
   A. Sculptures can be made of wood.
   B. Paintings are always one color.
   C. There are sections in some museums for children.
   D. People who paint are called artists.

 #50087 Reading Comprehension—Level B

# Camping

## Before Reading

- Have you ever been camping?
- What do you like to do with your family?

## During Reading

- Where does the family go camping?
- What is Dad's favorite activity?

## After Reading

- What does the family do around the campfire?
- Do you think the family has a good time?

## Vocabulary

breezy: lightly windy

shore: the land near a lake or ocean

campfire: a small outdoor fire, sometimes in a pit

I love to camp with my family. We camp by the lake. Dad sets up the tent. He sits at the picnic bench and reads all day. He loves to read in the shade. Later he will tell us stories.

Mom rents a paddle boat. Out we go. We push the pedals with our feet to move around. The water makes a noise. Splish. Splash. It is breezy out on the lake. We are far from the shore.

At night we sit around the campfire. It glows bright orange. It is time for stories. Dad tells a spooky story that scares us. Then he tells a silly story. He can make us laugh for hours. Mom and I tell stories too.

We go to bed early. We lie side by side and sleep. We will not wake up until the sun hits our tent early in the morning.

# Analyze Plot Structure

Think about "Camping." What does it tell about? Fill the chart with details from the story. Tell about the beginning, middle, and end.

**Beginning**

**Main Idea:** Dad sets up a tent.

**Details:** _____

_____

_____

**Middle**

**Main Idea:** Mom rents a paddle boat.

**Details:** _____

_____

_____

**End**

**Main Idea:** We tell stories at night.

**Details:** _____

_____

_____

# Identify Cause and Effect

Read each sentence on the left. Choose a detail from the story to show what happens next. Draw a line to connect the left and right sentences.

**Causes**

Dad tells a funny story.

We push the pedals in the boat.

Dad tells a spooky story.

The sun will hit our tent.

**Effects**

The boat moves.

We will wake up.

He gives us a fright.

We laugh for hours.

Draw one of the scenes from above.

# Comprehension Practice

Circle the letter of the best answer.

1. Where does the story take place?
   A. at the beach
   B. in the mountains
   C. in the desert
   D. at a lake

2. What does Dad like to do best?
   A. rent a paddle boat
   B. read in the shade
   C. set up a tent
   D. go to bed early

3. What makes the water splash?
   A. The boat moves the water.
   B. There is a thunderstorm.
   C. It is hot out.
   D. It is shady.

4. How do you know the family shares a tent?
   A. The tent is in the shade.
   B. They go to bed early.
   C. They laugh for hours.
   D. They lie side by side.

5. What does this story show the reader?
   A. Parents should have time away from their kids.
   B. Camping is fun but too much work.
   C. It is nice when families spend time together.
   D. Brothers and sisters never get along.

6. What does **rent** mean in the story?
   A. to pay to use
   B. to win
   C. to steal
   D. to take

7. When does Dad tell stories?
   A. as soon as everyone wakes up
   B. when the kids are asleep
   C. late at night around the campfire
   D. on their way back home

8. What happens when the pedals are pushed in a paddle boat?
   A. The siren goes off.
   B. It puts on the brakes.
   C. The boat moves.
   D. Nothing happens.

# High Dive

Terry is up high. She is on the high dive. She feels her palms get sweaty. Her knees begin to wobble. She sees the pool water far below. Far, far below. She does not want to dive.

"You can do it!" her friends shout. Terry sees the ladder. She wants to go back down. She wants to feel her feet on the ground. She does not want to dive.

"Dive, dive, dive!" her sister Karen shouts. Karen likes to dive. Terry's friends like to dive too. It is Terry's turn now. But she does not want to jump.

Terry is scared to dive. She is scared to go back down the ladder too. What if her friends laugh at her? She knows it is best to jump. She goes to the edge of the diving board. She closes her eyes. She dives!

## Vocabulary

dive: to jump head first into water

wobble: to shake back and forth

edge: the line or border where one thing ends and another begins

# Make Predictions

As you read "High Dive," think about how the story will end. What will Terry do? Draw a picture of Terry on a diving board. Draw what you think will happen. Write a title for your picture. Write two sentences about your picture.

_____

_____

_____

_____

_____

# Make Inferences

Answer these story questions and tell how you got your answer.

1. Where is Terry? How do you know?

   _____

   _____


2. How does Terry feel about diving? How do you know?

   _____

   _____


3. How do her friends feel about diving? How do you know?

   _____

   _____


4. Why does Terry close her eyes before diving? How do you know?

   _____

   _____

# Comprehension Practice

Circle the letter of the best answer.

1. Where does the story take place?
   A. at school
   B. at a pool
   C. at summer camp
   D. at the market

2. Why do Terry's knees wobble?
   A. She is cold.
   B. The wind blows them.
   C. She is excited.
   D. She is scared.

3. What do Terry's friends want her to do?
   A. go down the ladder
   B. swim in a race
   C. jump
   D. go home

4. How do you think Terry will feel after her dive?
   A. shy
   B. proud
   C. sad
   D. mad

5. What is Terry's problem in the story?
   A. She is afraid to dive into the pool.
   B. Her bathing suit is cuter than everyone else's.
   C. The pool water is too cold.
   D. She doesn't know how to swim.

6. What does the word **dive** mean?
   A. to go in through the side
   B. to jump in head first
   C. to swim in slowly
   D. to shake a lot

7. Do you think Terry will dive again?
   A. No, because she climbed down the ladder.
   B. Yes, because she survived her first dive.
   C. Yes, because Mom will make her.
   D. No, because her friends will laugh.

8. What is Terry likely thinking about when she is on the diving board?
   A. if the water will be too warm
   B. how fast she can climb down that ladder
   C. whether she should jump or not
   D. why her friends are so mean

# The New Glove

Takeshi was the best baseball player in his class. He played shortstop. He could jump higher than anyone to catch a fly ball. He always ran fast to pick up speedy grounders. Nobody liked to go to bat when Takeshi was in the field.

But one day his game was not the same. He could not catch the ball. He dropped it every time. He did not play well the next day or the day after that. He began to feel gloomy. He asked his dad for help.

"Let's see," said Dad. He watched Takeshi play. He watched him closely. "I think I know the problem. Look at your glove. It is too small. You have grown!"

Takeshi looked at his mitt. It was true. He had grown. Dad took him to the store to buy a larger glove. The next time Takeshi went out on the field, he was the star player again.

## Before Reading

- What kinds of sports do you like to play?
- How does your game change as you grow?

## During Reading

- What skills do you need to play baseball?
- Why might Takeshi feel gloomy?

## After Reading

- What happens when you get too big for your clothes or shoes?
- What advice would you give to Takeshi?

## Vocabulary

shortstop: a field position in baseball between second and third base

grounders: the type of baseball hit that rolls fast on the ground

gloomy: sad; unhappy

# Use Prior Knowledge and Make Connections

Read "The New Glove." Connect what you read with what you already know about baseball. Answer the following questions.

1. Can you play baseball by yourself? Why or why not?

_____

_____

2. What equipment do you need to play a baseball game?

_____

_____

3. What makes a good baseball player?

_____

_____

4. How can somebody improve how he or she plays?

_____

_____

# Problem Solving

What trouble does Takeshi face in this story? How does he solve his problem? Write your answers in the chart.

| Problem | Solution |
|---------|----------|
|         |          |

# Comprehension Practice

Circle the letter of the best answer.

1. In what sport is Takeshi a star player?
   A. basketball
   B. softball
   C. dodgeball
   D. baseball

2. What position does Takeshi play?
   A. shortstop
   B. catcher
   C. first base
   D. pitcher

3. What is Takeshi's main problem?
   A. He is too old to play baseball.
   B. His glove does not fit him anymore.
   C. His dad does not allow him to play.
   D. A new kid plays better than him.

4. How do you think Takeshi feels about his new glove?
   A. He is shy that he has grown.
   B. He is glad to have a glove that fits.
   C. He is mad that the new glove is too small.
   D. He is upset to lose his old glove.

5. What is this story mainly about?
   A. a boy and his father who start a baseball team
   B. kids who grow up too fast
   C. a boy and his father who solve a problem
   D. the rules of baseball

6. Which phrase is the same as **grounders**?
   A. a baseball hit that rolls fast on the ground
   B. what you can buy at the meat store
   C. a skateboard trick
   D. a fly ball

7. Why does Takeshi need a new glove?
   A. He wants two gloves.
   B. His hand has gotten bigger.
   C. He is the star player.
   D. He wants a fancy blue one.

8. Who does Takeshi ask for help?
   A. his glove
   B. his friend Billy
   C. his coach
   D. his dad

# Snack Time

Popcorn is a delicious treat. You can make it at home with your family. Before you do, you need to buy popcorn kernels. You can get them at the store. Kernels are really small. They are hard and yellow. They are too hard to eat! If you try one, it will not taste good. You have to cook them.

First, put the kernels in a pot. Next, add cooking oil. Cover the pot with a lid. Have your mom or dad turn on the heat. Do not stand too close. You can hear the popcorn from far away.

The kernels jump in the hot oil. They start to rattle. Pop, pop, pop! Each kernel gets big and fluffy. Now you have a tasty treat!

## Before Reading

- What kind of snacks do you like best?
- What foods do you like to make with your family?

## During Reading

- What do you have to do before you make popcorn?
- What is the first step in making popcorn?

## After Reading

- Why do you need your mom and dad to help you?
- Why is "popcorn" a good name for this snack?

## Vocabulary

delicious: when something tastes good

kernels: small, hard pieces of uncooked corn

rattle: a noise made by objects hitting together

# Identify Main Idea and Supporting Details

In "Snack Time," you learned about how to make popcorn. You also learned a lot about what popcorn is made from—kernels. In the web below, write all the things you learned about kernels in the outer boxes.

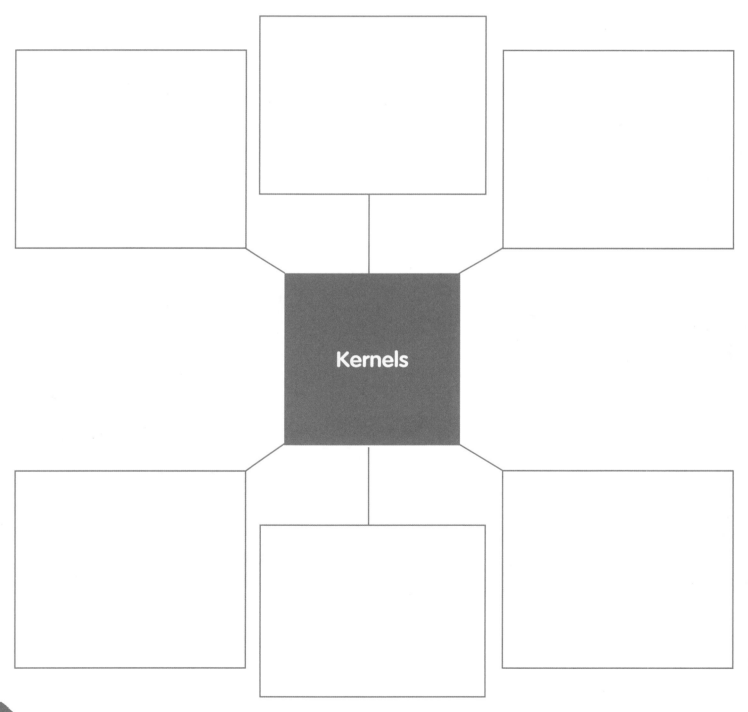

# Identify Sequence

"Snack Time" tells how to make popcorn. It tells what to do in order. Number the steps to show the right order. Reread the steps to check your answers.

_____ Add cooking oil.

_____ Put the kernels in a pot.

_____ Buy popcorn kernels at the store.

_____ Turn on the heat and cook the kernels.

_____ Cover the pot with a lid.

_____ Enjoy a tasty treat!

Draw a picture showing one of these steps.

# Comprehension Practice

Circle the letter of the best answer.

1.  Where can you get popcorn kernels?
    A.  at the beach
    B.  in the park
    C.  at the store
    D.  near the pool

2.  What do you need to make popcorn?
    A.  peanut butter and jelly
    B.  a bowl and a spoon
    C.  dish soap and a towel
    D.  a pot, oil, and a stove

3.  What happens to the hot kernels?
    A.  They get wet.
    B.  They start to pop.
    C.  They turn green.
    D.  They disappear.

4.  How do you know the popcorn is ready?
    A.  It gets big and fluffy.
    B.  It sticks to the wall.
    C.  It is hard and yellow.
    D.  It tastes like pizza.

5.  What could be another title for this story?
    A.  Grow Your Own Kernels
    B.  Hot Cooking Tips
    C.  How to Make Popcorn
    D.  Popcorn: A Nutritious Treat

6.  Which word means the same as **delicious**?
    A.  yucky
    B.  tasty
    C.  bitter
    D.  dumb

7.  What do popcorn kernels look like?
    A.  They are big and fluffy.
    B.  They are flat and round.
    C.  They are small and yellow.
    D.  They are long and black.

8.  What do you do after you add the cooking oil?
    A.  turn the heat on very high
    B.  add butter to the popcorn
    C.  put a lid on the pot
    D.  stand close to the stove

# Ants and Bees

Ants and bees are both insects. They both have three body parts. They both have six legs.

Ants and bees live in groups. The groups are called colonies. Many ants can live in one group. Many bees can live in one group. Ants and bees have queens. The queen ant lays the eggs. The queen bee lays the eggs. That is all the queen ant does. That is all the queen bee does. They sure have a lot in common!

Ants can be yellow, brown, red, or black. They are small. Ants will eat anything. Ants make their nests under the dirt. A nest is a home for many ants. Ants eat seeds, fruits, flowers, or small bugs.

Some bees are black. They have stripes. These bees are honeybees. They are small. They make their hives above ground. A hive is a home for many bees. Honeybees suck nectar or pollen from flowers. They use the nectar or pollen to make honey. Next time you enjoy some honey, thank a bee!

## Before Reading
- What is an insect?
- Do you like insects? Why?

## During Reading
- What is a colony?
- What color can an ant be?

## After Reading
- What makes an insect an insect?
- What do the queen insects do?

## Vocabulary
insect: an animal with three body parts and six legs

colony: a group of ants or bees

nectar: the sweet juice from a flower

common: same; alike

# Ask Questions

When you read a selection, you might have questions about the topic. Asking questions helps you learn more about the topic and shows that you are interested in what you are reading. After reading the story "Ants and Bees," write down a question that you have for each one of the topics.

| Topic | Question |
|---|---|
| **1.** Insects | |
| **2.** Ants | |
| **3.** Bees | |
| **4.** Colonies | |
| **5.** Nectar | |

# Compare and Contrast

To compare two items, find something that is the same or similar about both of them. To contrast two items, find something that is different about them. Complete the chart comparing and contrasting ants and bees.

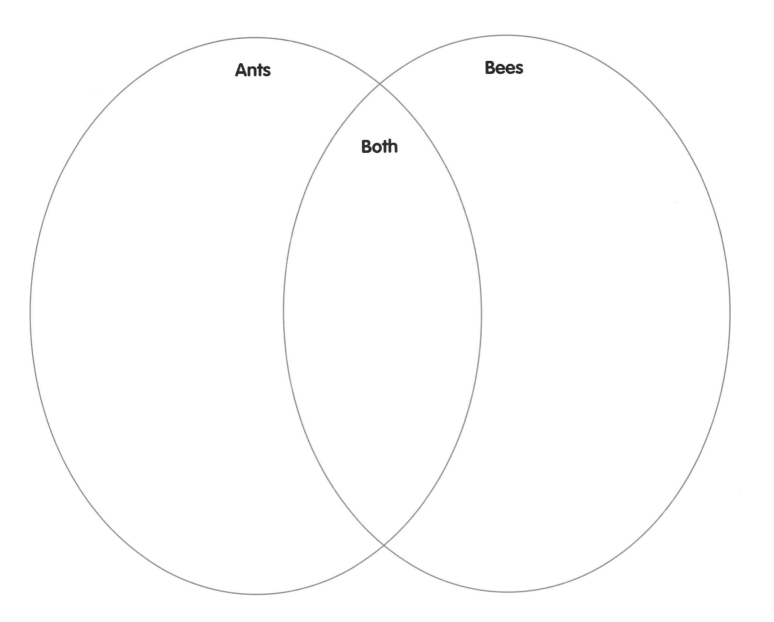

# Comprehension Practice

Circle the letter of the best answer.

1. How many legs does an insect have?
   A. three
   B. four
   C. five
   D. six

2. What markings are on a bee's body?
   A. dots
   B. stripes
   C. checks
   D. plaid

3. What does the queen ant or queen bee do?
   A. make the nest
   B. do the work
   C. lay eggs
   D. protect the other ants or bees

4. What is used to make honey?
   A. dirt
   B. nests
   C. eggs
   D. nectar

5. Which of the following is NOT important to the topic of this story?
   A. Ants and bees are insects.
   B. Ants and bees live in colonies.
   C. Ants will eat anything.
   D. Hens lay eggs too.

6. When two things have something in **common**, they _____.
   A. are completely different
   B. share characteristics
   C. are boring
   D. bell

7. Which is the most logical question to ask about ants and bees?
   A. What colors are bees besides black?
   B. How are butterflies like bees?
   C. Why is honey so sticky?
   D. Where are the king ants and bees?

8. How are ants' and bees' homes different?
   A. Ants live above the dirt, bees live under the dirt.
   B. Ants live in nests, bees live in hives.
   C. Ants live in flowers, bees live in bushes.
   D. Bees live in nests just like ants.

# Put a Hat on Your Head

There are all kinds of hats. There are many reasons for wearing hats. All kinds of people have hats.

There are hats for safety. These hats are called helmets. Firefighters have helmets. The helmet keeps them safe if something falls on them. Kids have helmets too. The helmets keep them safe if they fall off their bikes, roller blades, or skateboards.

There are also hats for jobs. Cowboys have hats. The hats keep the sun off their heads. Bakers have hats to keep their hair out of the food.

Some hats are called caps. Caps can keep your head warm. They can also keep the sun out of your eyes. Some hats are on jackets. These are called hoods. They keep people warm when it's cold outside.

There are even hats for fun. There are party hats. They have lots of colors. Maybe you've worn one at a birthday party! There are clown hats. Clown hats have pom-pom balls on the tips. There are silly hats. Mouse ears are silly hats. Which kind of hat do you like to wear?

## Before Reading

- What kinds of hats have you worn?
- What kind of hat would you like to wear? Why?

## During Reading

- Why are some hats hard?
- Which hats keep people warm?

## After Reading

- What are the reasons for wearing a hat?
- What kinds of jobs require special hats?

## Vocabulary

hat: a piece of clothing worn on the head

helmet: a hard hat, used for protection

baker: someone who prepares food, usually desserts

# Identify Main Idea and Supporting Details

Read "Put a Hat on Your Head." The title helps you know what the article is mainly about—hats. Each paragraph tells you about a different kind of hat. Fill in the missing details in the chart below for each kind of hat.

| Kind of Hat | Reason for Wearing the Hat | People Who Wear the Hat |
|---|---|---|
| Helmet | | |
| Baker's hat | | |
| Cap | | |
| Fun hat | | |

# Use Prior Knowledge and Make Connections

The facts you know about one topic can sometimes help you learn and understand facts about a new topic. Complete the K-W-L chart on "Put a Hat on Your Head."

| What I Know About Hats | What I Want to Know About Hats | What I Learned About Hats |
|---|---|---|
|  |  |  |
|  |  |  |
|  |  |  |
|  |  |  |

# Comprehension Practice

Circle the letter of the best answer.

1. What kind of hat is worn when riding a bike?
   A. helmet
   B. cap
   C. cowboy hat
   D. mouse ears

2. Who wears a hat to keep their hair out of the food?
   A. a baker
   B. a plumber
   C. a clown
   D. a firefighter

3. Why do people wear hoods?
   A. for safety
   B. to keep warm
   C. for fun
   D. to be silly

4. Who would most likely wear a silly hat?
   A. a police officer
   B. someone out in the sun
   C. a clown
   D. someone playing in the snow

5. This story addresses the issue of _____.
   A. uniforms firefighters wear
   B. how to keep warm during winter
   C. why people wear silly hats
   D. different hats and their functions

6. Why is a **helmet** worn?
   A. to make a fashion statement
   B. to keep the head secure
   C. to keep the ears warm
   D. to perform crazy stunts

7. What do clown hats sometimes have on them?
   A. pom-poms
   B. buckles
   C. goggles
   D. pop tarts

8. Which is something a baker makes?
   A. airplanes
   B. coats
   C. pies
   D. tires

# To the Zoo

Friday was field trip day. Miss Russell was taking her second-grade class to the zoo. She got to school early to get the name tags ready.

At 9:00 the children came into the classroom. Miss Russell handed out the name tags. "Everyone choose a partner," she directed. "Then we'll get on the bus!"

The 24 children got on the bus and sat two in a seat with their partners. Three parents joined the class to help. The bus sure was noisy! They sang songs and talked excitedly about the animals they hoped they would see.

When the bus arrived at the zoo, Miss Russell said, "We will all stay together and follow the trail to see the animals."

Four hours later, after they saw 22 different animals, Miss Russell said, "It's 2:00. Time to go back to school!" The class climbed back on the bus to return to school. This time, there were not many sounds on the bus, except the sounds of snoring!

## Before Reading

- Have you ever gone on a field trip?
- How do children travel on a field trip?

## During Reading

- How many people are going on the bus, not including the bus driver?
- What day of the week is the field trip?

## After Reading

- Was the bus noisier on the way to or on the way back from the trip?
- How many animals did the class see?

## Vocabulary

bus: a large vehicle on wheels that carries many people

zoo: a place where people can see many different animals

partner: a person who stays with another person

# Identify Sequence

Read "To the Zoo" and then read the sentences below. Put them in the order they happened in the story.

Each child chose a partner.

Miss Russell made name tags.

There was the sound of snoring on the bus.

They followed the trail to see the animals.

1. _____

2. _____

3. _____

_____

4. _____

_____

Draw a picture of a part of the trip.

# Identify Cause and Effect

Think about "To the Zoo." Read each event below. Write what caused each thing to happen.

1. **Effect:** Miss Russell got to school early.

   **Cause:** _____

2. **Effect:** The bus was noisy!

   **Cause:** _____

3. **Effect:** Miss Russell was taking the class to the zoo.

   **Cause:** _____

4. **Effect:** The children climbed back on the bus.

   **Cause:** _____

# Comprehension Practice

Circle the letter of the best answer.

1. Who did each child sit with on the bus?
   A. Miss Russell
   B. the principal
   C. a partner
   D. each child sat alone

2. Why did three parents go along?
   A. They had never been to the zoo.
   B. They went to help.
   C. They won a contest.
   D. It was their birthday.

3. What did the children do on the bus on the way to the zoo?
   A. ate lunch
   B. sang songs and talked
   C. talked about bus safety
   D. looked at 22 animals

4. What did they do at 2:00?
   A. got back on the bus
   B. visited the zoo store
   C. ate lunch
   D. had a fire drill

5. What is this story mainly about?
   A. a trip to an amusement park
   B. a trip with the whole school
   C. a second-grade field trip to the zoo
   D. a second-grade class gets a new teacher

6. Which word does NOT go with its definition?
   A. **classroom**—a place where students have recess
   B. **bus**—a large vehicle on wheels that carries many people
   C. **partner**—a person who stays with another person
   D. **zoo**—a place where people can see many different animals

7. What did the children likely do before they got on the bus?
   A. They wrote a report about the zoo.
   B. They made their name tags.
   C. They picked their partners.
   D. They saw a video about animals.

8. Why did Miss Russell hand out name tags?
   A. to add color to the students' clothes
   B. so strangers at the zoo could talk to them
   C. the students don't know their own names
   D. so each student could be easily identified

# Land, Sea, and Air

### Before Reading

- What kinds of animals can you name?

- Where do these animals live?

### During Reading

- How do sea animals move in the water?

- Why do you think birds spend so much time in the air?

### After Reading

- Why do you think some animals have wings and some have fins?

- What is your favorite kind of animal?

### Vocabulary

soar: to fly high

wrinkle: to show folds and creases

fins: a body part used for moving in water

Animals are all around us. They live on land, swim in the sea, and soar high above us in the air.

Land animals stay on the ground like we do. Some, like cats and dogs, live in our homes. Think about horses, monkeys, and kangaroos. They do not look the same at all. But they are all types of land animals. People are land animals too!

Sea animals stay in the water. What would happen if you spent all day in the bath or pool? Your skin would wrinkle like a prune! Sea animals do better in water than they would on land. Many have fins to help them swim. Fish, sharks, and whales are all sea animals. They never stop swimming, even when they sleep.

Birds are animals that fly high in the air. They use their wings to fly to places other animals never see. They make their homes up in the trees. Eagles, parrots, and cranes are all types of air animals. They fly over land and sea and watch us from above.

# Classify/Categorize

Read "Land, Sea, and Air." Write the names of these animals where they belong on the chart. Think of another animals to add to each list.

| | | | | | |
|---|---|---|---|---|---|
| horses | parrots | sharks | dogs | cranes | monkeys |
| whales | fish | cats | eagles | kangaroos | |

| Land Animals | Sea Animals | Air Animals |
|---|---|---|
| | | |

# Compare and Contrast

What does "Land, Sea, and Air" tell us about animals? Reread the story. Compare and contrast land and sea animals. How are they alike? How are they different? Add details of your own.

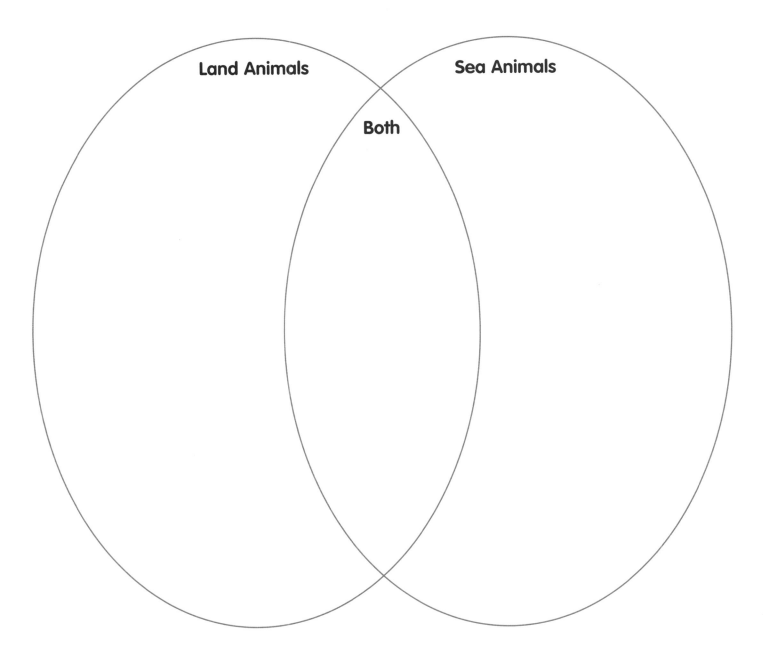

**Land Animals**

**Sea Animals**

**Both**

# Comprehension Practice

Circle the letter of the best answer.

1. What is this story mainly about?
   A. land animals
   B. sea animals
   C. air animals
   D. animals all around us

2. Which of these animals lives in the sea?
   A. monkey
   B. whale
   C. dog
   D. parrot

3. What would happen if you stayed in water all day?
   A. Your skin would wrinkle.
   B. You would grow fins.
   C. You would become a fish.
   D. You would make your home in the trees.

4. Which animal can fly high up in the sky?
   A. an eagle
   B. a monkey
   C. a fish
   D. a whale

5. What could this story also be called?
   A. Animals Everywhere You Go
   B. When Animals Attack
   C. Animals Looking Down
   D. Traveling By Sea

6. When skin **folds and creases**, it becomes _____.
   A. smooth
   B. wrinkled
   C. youthful
   D. feathery

7. An animal can have all but which one of the following?
   A. fins
   B. wings
   C. two feet
   D. a wooden tail

8. Which of the following correctly contrasts horses and cats?
   A. Horses can fly, cats can't.
   B. Cats and horses are both land animals.
   C. Cats live in peoples' homes, horses do not.
   D. Horses look like giant cats.

# The Special Gift

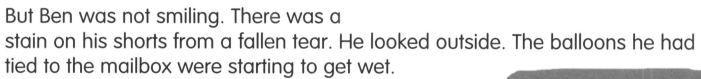

It was a very special day for Ben. It was his favorite day of the year. Today Ben was turning eight years old. He had invited ten friends to share the fun with him. They would arrive soon.

But Ben was not smiling. There was a stain on his shorts from a fallen tear. He looked outside. The balloons he had tied to the mailbox were starting to get wet.

Ben thought of the games he wanted to play in the backyard. His dad had found sacks for three-legged races. "Now," Ben whispered, "that's ruined."

A car drove into the driveway. His friend Danny jumped out and yelled, "Happy Birthday!" He handed Ben a present. Another car arrived. Ben's mother announced, "Oh look. It's Alex. And look, Ben," she continued, "another very special guest has come out for your party."

Ben turned his head and looked at the sky. He covered his eyes from the bright light. He felt the heat on his face. The guest he had been waiting and hoping for had come to his party. "It's going to be a great party after all!" Ben yelled.

## Before Reading

- When is your birthday?
- How do you celebrate your birthday?

## During Reading

- What is Ben worried about in the story?
- Where is Ben planning to have his party?

## After Reading

- Was Ben's birthday spoiled?
- Who was the special guest Ben was happy to see at his party?

## Vocabulary

special: something that does not happen every day

guest: someone who is invited to a party or an event

arrive: to reach a place

ruined: destroyed; wrecked

# Make Predictions

Read the following sentences from the story and predict what is going to happen for each.

**1.** Today Ben was turning eight years old. He had invited ten friends to share the fun with him.

_____

_____

**2.** But Ben was not smiling. There was a stain on his shorts from a fallen tear.

_____

_____

**3.** He looked outside. The balloons he had tied to the mailbox were starting to get wet.

_____

_____

**4.** Ben turned his head and looked at the sky. He covered his eyes from the bright light. He felt the heat on his face.

_____

_____

# Problem Solving

Read the story, "The Special Gift" and think about what is happening in it. Answer the questions below.

**1.** Ben has a problem. He is worried. What is he worried about?

_____

**2.** How could Ben solve his problem? What could he do if it rained all day?

_____

**3.** Draw a picture to show your idea and then explain it on the lines below.

_____

_____

_____

_____

# Comprehension Practice

Circle the letter of the best answer.

1. Why was it a special day for Ben?
   A. He lost his tooth.
   B. It was his birthday.
   C. He was moving to a new house.
   D. He got a puppy.

2. How many friends did Ben invite?
   A. five
   B. seven
   C. three
   D. ten

3. What was an activity Ben had planned?
   A. jump roping
   B. three–legged races
   C. water balloon fights
   D. a football game

4. Which guest had Ben been waiting for?
   A. the sun
   B. his friend Alex
   C. a neighbor
   D. his cousin Danny

5. What is Ben's problem in the story?
   A. He is afraid of getting old.
   B. He doesn't have a lot of presents to open.
   C. It's too hot to be outside all day.
   D. The weather is not good for his party.

6. What is another word for **ruined**?
   A. wet
   B. destroyed
   C. wrong
   D. solved

7. What do you think the weather will be for the birthday party?
   A. boiling
   B. snowy
   C. sunny
   D. rainy

8. What would be a good solution if the weather was bad?
   A. get wet
   B. go indoors
   C. cry
   D. cancel his birthday

 #50087 Reading Comprehension—Level B

# Making Maple Syrup

### Before Reading

- Have you ever eaten maple syrup?
- What do you put maple syrup on?

### During Reading

- What is the sugar water called before it becomes syrup?
- How does the sap change to syrup?

### After Reading

- What is the last thing that happens before syrup is sent to stores?
- Can you make syrup from any tree? Why or why not?

Many people eat maple syrup on their pancakes. Most people don't know that maple syrup comes from the sugar maple tree. There are many steps to follow when making syrup.

First, holes are drilled into the tree trunks. This does not hurt the trees. Spiles, or spouts, are placed in the holes and a bucket is placed below. The sugar water, also called sap, drips drop by drop into the bucket through the spile.

After sap is collected in the bucket, it is poured into a pot. Then the sap is boiled over a fire. As it boils and boils, the water that is part of the sap becomes steam and disappears. The liquid that is still in the pot becomes sweeter and changes to an orange-brown color.

The sap is now syrup. It is sweet and sticky. The syrup is poured through a filter and packed into cans, bottles, or plastic containers. Then it is shipped to grocery stores for people to buy. You will see it on the store shelf. It has traveled far to get from the tree to your table!

### Vocabulary

sap: watery liquid that flows through a tree

syrup: thick, sweet, sticky liquid

spout: a tube or pipe for liquid to go through

# Identify Sequence

Read "Making Maple Syrup." Think about the order in which things happen to make maple syrup. List the steps of the process in order below.

| Steps to Make Maple Syrup |
| --- |
| 1. |
| 2. |
| 3. |
| 4. |
| 5. |
| 6. |

*#50087 Reading Comprehension—Level B*                                © *Teacher Created Materials*

# Fact and Opinion

A **fact** is something real. It can be proven. An **opinion** is what a person thinks or feels. Read each sentence below about "Making Maple Syrup." Circle "Fact" if it is true. Circle "Opinion" if it is how someone feels.

1. Trees should not have holes drilled in them.

   Fact                    Opinion

2. Sap comes out of the tree drop by drop.

   Fact                    Opinion

3. Maple syrup comes from the sugar maple tree.

   Fact                    Opinion

4. Maple syrup does not taste good .

   Fact                    Opinion

5. The best maple syrup comes in cans.

   Fact                    Opinion

6. Maple syrup is sweet and sticky.

   Fact                    Opinion

# Comprehension Practice

Circle the letter of the best answer.

1. Where does maple syrup come from?
   A. cows
   B. candy
   C. trees
   D. butter

2. Syrup begins as_____.
   A. sap
   B. sugar
   C. sun
   D. cream

3. After the sap comes out of the tree it is ready to_____.
   A. ship to the store
   B. boil over a fire
   C. freeze
   D. eat

4. What is one way that syrup is NOT packed?
   A. in paper bags
   B. in cans
   C. in plastic containers
   D. in bottles

5. What is the main idea of this story?
   A. the many uses for syrup
   B. where maple trees originated
   C. destroying trees
   D. how maple syrup is made

6. What word signifies a tube that syrup flows through?
   A. a garden hose
   B. a spile
   C. a fire hose
   D. a faucet

7. What is the first step in making maple syrup?
   A. Syrup is poured into cans.
   B. Sap is collected in buckets.
   C. Holes are drilled into tree trunks.
   D. Sap is boiled over a fire.

8. Which of the following is an opinion about maple syrup?
   A. Maple syrup is yummier than chocolate!
   B. Maple syrup comes from the sugar maple tree.
   C. Maple syrup can be eaten on pancakes.
   D. Maple syrup has a sweet taste.

# Second-grade Mikes

It was the first day of second grade. Mike Brown was excited. His teacher's name was Miss Clark. He already knew her from school.

Class started at 9:00. The first thing they were told was to choose a desk. Then Miss Clark said, "I will read your names. When you hear your name, raise your hand and say 'Here'."

"Anna, Calvin, Kristen, Lucy," she called. Mike waited for his name. "Marcia, Mike," Miss Clark said out loud. Mike Brown raised his left hand and called out, "Here!" But his voice sounded very loud.

Mike Brown looked around and saw another boy raising his right hand. "Oh my!" Miss Clark said. "It seems we have two Mikes in our class. Let's see how we'll tell them apart."

All of the kids looked at the two Mikes. The two Mikes looked at each other. "Both boys are seven years old and are wearing shorts. Both boys are wearing long-sleeved shirts. Hmmm," she said. Mike Brown was nervous. How would they not get mixed up?

Then the teacher said, "I know! Mike Holt has hazel eyes, and Mike Brown has black eyes. So Mike H. and Mike B., welcome to second grade!" Both Mikes giggled and knew that it was going to be a fun year.

## Before Reading

- How do you feel on the first day of school each year?
- Do you know someone with the same name as yours?

## During Reading

- Why does Miss Clark ask them to raise their hands and say "Here"?
- In what order does Miss Clark call students' names?

## After Reading

- How would the story be different if they both had black eyes?
- Besides the color of their eyes, give another reason Miss Clark chose Mike H. and Mike B. as their new names.

## Vocabulary

nervous: uneasy or fearful about something

choose: to pick out something

giggle: to laugh with short, high sounds

# Compare and Contrast

Think about what you know about the two boys named Mike. They are alike in many ways. They are also different. In the diagram below, list things that are only true of Mike B. in the left circle. List things in the right circle that are only true of Mike H. In the center area, list things that are true of both Mikes.

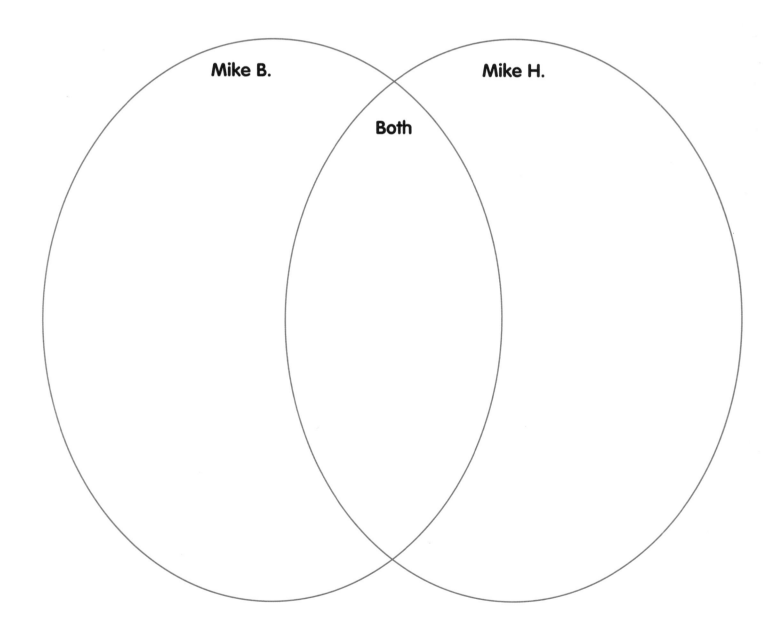

# Analyze Plot Structure

A plot is a group of things that happen in a story. A plot has a beginning, a middle, and an end. Read "Second-grade Mikes" and tell the beginning, the middle, and the end of the story.

**Beginning:** _____

_____

_____

**Middle:** _____

_____

_____

**End:** _____

_____

_____

# Comprehension Practice

Circle the letter of the best answer.

1. What is Mike excited about?
   A. the beginning of summer
   B. a camping trip
   C. the first day of school
   D. meeting his teacher for the first time

2. How old are the two Mikes?
   A. seven
   B. five
   C. nine
   D. two

3. Why is Mike B. nervous?
   A. He doesn't know who his teacher is going to be.
   B. There was no chair left for him to sit on.
   C. He's worried that he and Mike H. will get mixed up.
   D. He was late to school on the first day.

4. What was the first thing they did in class?
   A. find a desk
   B. write their names
   C. have recess
   D. tell about their summer

5. What could another title for this story be?
   A. Which Mike Is Which?
   B. Everyone Loves Miss Clark
   C. First Grade Blues
   D. Recess Fun

6. If you are **nervous**, what are you?
   A. noisy
   B. hungry
   C. a little afraid
   D. super confident

7. What is different between the two Mikes?
   A. the color of their eyes
   B. the length of their shirts
   C. their classroom
   D. their teacher's name

8. Why did Mike Brown already know who the teacher was?
   A. Miss Clark is his mom.
   B. He met her at the store.
   C. Miss Clark came to his house before school.
   D. He already knew her from school.

 #50087 Reading Comprehension—Level B

# Fluffy Fun

It was the first warm Saturday in a long time. It had been a long cold winter, and it was finally over. Maria was happy for two reasons. First, it was the weekend, so there was no school. Second, there were big, fluffy, white clouds in the pretty blue sky.

Maria grabbed her drawing pad. She grabbed her pencil. She went outside. She put her drawing things down. She lay down on her back on the grass. She looked up to the sky and felt the warm sun on her face. She smiled at what she saw.

Up to the right of her, Maria saw a horse. It had a long white mane and flowing tail. In the sky over the barn, a clown smiled down at her. He had a big round nose and pointed ears. "Yes!" Maria shouted out loud. "That's what I will draw."

Maria took her pencil and sketched the outline of the clown on the white drawing paper. She peeked up from time to time to check the shape of the cloud. Then she drew some more.

"Perfect!" Maria said with pride. "Now I will go inside and add color. Then I will come out and do it again!"

## Before Reading

- What do you do when the weather is warm?
- What kinds of pictures do you like to draw?

## During Reading

- Why is Maria so happy?
- Why does Maria lay down on the grass?

## After Reading

- What was Maria looking at in the sky?
- What did Maria do with what she saw in the sky?

## Vocabulary

sketch: to make a quick drawing

mane: long hair along the top and sides of the neck on an animal

peek: to look quickly

# Make Inferences

In "Fluffy Fun," some facts are not directly stated. You can infer, or use details in the story, to draw conclusions. Make inferences to answer these questions.

1. What season is it? How do you know?

   _____

   _____

2. Does Maria have a good imagination? How do you know?

   _____

   _____

3. Where does Maria live? How do you know?

   _____

   _____

4. Could this story be real or is it make-believe? What do you think?

   _____

   _____

# Visualize

Think about the clouds Maria saw in the sky above her house. Think about clouds you have seen in the sky. Have you ever seen a cloud that looks like something else? Make a picture in your mind of a fluffy white cloud in the sky. Draw the picture of what you see in your mind. Does it look like something else — an animal or something else that is familiar? Make a picture using a cloud from your imagination or one you have seen before. Give your picture a title and then describe it on the lines below.

_____

_____

_____

_____

_____

# Comprehension Practice

Circle the letter of the best answer.

1. Where does this story take place?
   A. in a barn
   B. at a school
   C. in a yard
   D. in a bedroom

2. What two things did Maria see in the sky?
   A. a dog and a cat
   B. a clown and a horse
   C. a horse and a cow
   D. a clown and a house

3. What are the shapes in the sky made of?
   A. clouds
   B. planes
   C. birds
   D. lights

4. What will Maria do when she goes inside?
   A. tell a story
   B. paint a horse
   C. write a poem
   D. color the clown

5. What is the main topic about?
   A. a girl who likes to sketch pictures
   B. a girl who flies a kite
   C. a boy who mows the grass
   D. a girl that can ride her bike

6. What did Maria do when she **peeked** at the sky?
   A. frowned
   B. yelled
   C. smiled
   D. looked quickly

7. What can you infer about Maria from the story?
   A. She does not have a good imagination.
   B. She gets bored easily.
   C. She is a creative and artistic person.
   D. She is good at telling funny stories.

8. How does the author help the reader visualize the clouds?
   A. by saying that they are big, fluffy, and white
   B. by comparing the shapes of the clouds to real-life things
   C. none of the above
   D. both A and B

# Bump in the Night

Randy woke up in a fright. He had heard a noise from outside. He wanted to tell his parents about it, but he was scared to walk down the hall to their room. He crept quietly over to his door. He peered around to look down the hall. It was dark at this time of night. The shadows from the window made the hall look extra long.

Randy would have gone back to bed if he had not heard the noise again. Bang! Rattle! Thump! What could it be? It sounded like somebody banging on pots and pans. He took a deep breath for courage and then ran down the hall. He burst into his parents' room and they woke with a start.

"What's going on?" said Dad.

"Why are you up?" said Mom.

Randy told them about the noise. The three of them listened quietly. There was not a sound for several minutes. All of a sudden—Bang! Rattle! Thump!

Dad grinned a goofy grin. "I know what that is," he said. He went out to the side of the house and returned with Maggie, their cat. "She was on the trash cans again." Randy went back to bed. He slept well the whole night with Maggie by his side.

## Before Reading

- What sounds do you hear during the day?
- What sounds can you hear at night?

## During Reading

- Why is Randy afraid to go down the hall?
- Why does Dad grin?

## After Reading

- What causes the hall to look extra long?
- Do you think Randy will hear the noise again? Why or why not?

## Vocabulary

crept: walked sneakily and quietly

courage: bravery

a start: a jump or twitch

# Make Predictions

As you read "Bump in the Night," think about how the story will end. What is causing all that noise? Write your guess below. Then draw a picture that shows what happened. Include details in your drawing that show how the noise was made.

What is causing the noise?

_____

_____

_____

# Identify Cause and Effect

The **cause** tells why something happened. The **effect** is what happens as a result of something. Draw a line to connect each cause on the left with its effect on the right.

| Causes | Effects |
| --- | --- |
| Randy hears a noise. | They wake with a start. |
| The hall is dark and long. | She makes a loud banging noise. |
| Maggie is on the trash cans. | Randy is afraid to walk down the hall. |
| Randy bursts into his parents' room. | He wakes up in a fright. |

Draw a scene from the story.

# Comprehension Practice

Circle the letter of the best answer.

1. Why does Randy wake up in a fright?
   A. He hears a loud noise.
   B. The shadows from the window scare him.
   C. Somebody bangs on pots and pans.
   D. It is dark in his room.

2. Which happens first?
   A. Randy runs down the hall.
   B. Randy wakes his parents.
   C. Randy takes a deep breath.
   D. Randy goes back to sleep.

3. Why do Randy's parents wake with a start?
   A. They forgot to take the trash out.
   B. Randy bursts into their room.
   C. They hear a noise from the kitchen.
   D. Randy yells from his bedroom.

4. What happens after Randy tells his parents about the noise?
   A. They take a deep breath for courage.
   B. They tell Randy to go back to bed.
   C. The shadows from the window make the hall look long.
   D. There is not a sound for several minutes.

5. What is "Bump in the Night" about?
   A. a boy who walks in his sleep
   B. a boy who has bad dreams
   C. a boy who loses his cat
   D. a boy is frightened by noises in the night

6. What happened when Randy **crept** over to his door?
   A. He reached for the doorknob.
   B. He walked without making noise.
   C. He ran fast and loudly.
   D. He put his hands over his eyes.

7. What will likely happen the next time Randy hears a noise at night?
   A. He won't feel as scared as he did this time.
   B. He will give his cat away because she's too noisy.
   C. He will get more scared and hide in the closet.
   D. He will sleep in his parent's bed for a week.

8. What made the hall look extra long at night?
   A. magic
   B. the mirror in the hall
   C. Randy's flashlight
   D. the shadows from the window

# Melissa's Special Pet

## Before Reading

- Do you have a pet in your home?
- What kinds of animals make good pets?

## During Reading

- Why might Melissa's Dad not want a pet?
- What extra chores do pets create?

## After Reading

- What kinds of pets would you want?
- How would you take care of a pet?

Melissa loves animals. She knows all the dogs on her street. She even names the birds she sees in the trees. Her greatest wish is to have her own pet, but Dad keeps saying no.

"Not even a goldfish?" asks Melissa.

"No pets!" exclaims Dad.

Grandpa has an idea. He invites Melissa over to play with his cats.

"Cats can be a lot of work," says Grandpa. "I feed them and give them water. I brush them and play with them every day."

"I guess," Melissa sulks. But she would not mind the extra work. She would take excellent care of a cat. She always helps Grandpa with his cats.

Grandpa smiles. He has a surprise in the kitchen. Melissa runs to see. She finds an adorable black-and-white kitten.

"You have a new pet?" she asks with excitement.

"No, you do!" exclaims Grandpa. "This kitten will live here with me and my cats, but she is yours. She is your own special pet!"

## Vocabulary

sulks: pouts unhappily

adorable: cute

exclaim: to say something loudly

# Analyze Plot Structure

Read "Melissa's Special Pet." Tell what happens in the beginning, middle, and end. Then draw a picture of Melissa with her pet.

**Beginning** _____

_____

_____

**Middle** _____

_____

_____

**End** _____

_____

_____

# Make Inferences

Answer these story questions and tell how you got your answer.

**1.** How does Dad feel about pets? How do you know?

_____

_____

_____

**2.** Why does Grandpa smile? How do you know?

_____

_____

_____

**3.** Will Melissa like her kitten? How do you know?

_____

_____

_____

**4.** Do you think Melissa will take good care of her pet? How do you know?

_____

_____

_____

# Comprehension Practice

Circle the letter of the best answer.

1. What is Melissa's greatest wish?
   A. to know all the dogs on her street
   B. to have her own special pet
   C. to buy a stuffed animal
   D. to live with Grandpa and his cats

2. Which animal is not mentioned in the story?
   A. dogs
   B. cats
   C. hamsters
   D. goldfish

3. What is Grandpa's surprise?
   A. He is giving Melissa his two cats.
   B. He will keep a kitten for Melissa.
   C. He lets Melissa brush his cats.
   D. He will take Melissa to the pet store.

4. How do you think Melissa feels about her surprise?
   A. happy
   B. worried
   C. upset
   D. proud

5. Which message is NOT provided in the story?
   A. Pets need food and water every day.
   B. Taking time to play with pets is also important.
   C. Pets require a lot of time and attention.
   D. Even irresponsible kids deserve a pet.

6. What is another word for **sulks**?
   A. mopes
   B. yells
   C. smiles
   D. exclaims

7. What does Melissa always do for her Grandpa?
   A. She helps him feed his dog.
   B. She makes him dinner.
   C. She helps him with his cats.
   D. She cleans his house.

8. Why does Melissa keep her new pet at Grandpa's house?
   A. He has a bigger yard.
   B. Only Grandpa knows how to train a pet.
   C. He has more money to buy cat food.
   D. Melissa's dad does not want any pets.

# The Birthday Cake

Dean's favorite treat was birthday cake. He loved cake with all his heart. But he had not had one crumb in a long time. And he could think of no birthdays coming up any time soon.

"That's okay," said Mom. "We can still make a birthday cake."

Dean was not so sure. "But who has a birthday in April?"

"It is always somebody's birthday," Mom said. "We can look in the paper." Mom helped Dean find the section in the paper that lists famous birthdays for each day. It was next to the comics.

"Today is April 23rd," said Mom. "It says William Shakespeare was born on this day."

"Who is he?" asked Dean.

"He wrote the world's most famous plays," said Mom.

That was good enough for Dean. "Let's celebrate!" he shouted with joy.

They made a cake and Mom wrote "Happy Birthday William" on it in red frosted letters. They each ate a slice. Dean did not know much about Shakespeare, but he felt they should celebrate his birthday with a cake every year.

# Problem Solving

Read "The Birthday Cake." What problem does Dean face in this story? How is his problem solved? Write your answers in the chart.

| Problem | Solution |
| --- | --- |
|  |  |

# Make Inferences

Answer these story questions and tell how you got your answer.

**1.** Has Dean ever tasted a birthday cake before? How do you know?

_____

_____

_____

**2.** Does Mom like cake? How do you know?

_____

_____

_____

**3.** Is Dean upset about Shakespeare's birthday? How do you know?

_____

_____

_____

**4.** Does Dean like the birthday cake they made? How do you know?

_____

_____

_____

# Comprehension Practice

Circle the letter of the best answer.

1. Which sentence from the story describes how Dean feels about cake?
   A. Dean was not so sure.
   B. He loved cake with all his heart.
   C. It was next to the comics.
   D. They each ate a slice.

2. What do you predict will happen next April 23rd?
   A. Mom and Dean will make Shakespeare a birthday cake.
   B. They will have a surprise party for Shakespeare.
   C. Dean will read all of Shakespeare's plays.
   D. Mom will check the newspaper to see whose birthday it is.

3. How do Mom and Dean celebrate Shakespeare's birthday?
   A. They invite their friends for a party.
   B. They decorate their home.
   C. They read one of his plays.
   D. They make a birthday cake.

4. Which story detail happens last?
   A. Mom tells Dean about Shakespeare.
   B. Mom and Dean look in the newspaper.
   C. Mom and Dean eat a slice of cake.
   D. Dean can think of no birthdays in April.

5. What is the main problem in the story?
   A. Mom does not want Dean to eat too much sugar.
   B. Dean really wants to eat his favorite treat, birthday cake.
   C. Mom wants vanilla frosting on the cake, but Dean wants chocolate.
   D. Dean is having trouble understanding Shakespeare's plays.

6. What is a **slice**?
   A. a whole
   B. a piece
   C. a knife
   D. a half

7. How does Mom solve Dean's problem?
   A. She makes up a fake birthday.
   B. She tells Dean that today is her birthday.
   C. She looks at famous birthdays in the paper.
   D. She buys him a cake at the bakery.

8. How do you know from the story that Shakespeare is famous?
   A. His birthday is listed in the newspaper.
   B. His name was in a movie.
   C. Mom found a cake with his name on it.
   D. Dean had to write a report about him for school.

# The Buzzer

Nick liked to play basketball more than anything. He played all the time. He even practiced with a little hoop in his bedroom. He played every night before bed.

Nick was playing in the championship game. His team, the Eagles, had 46 points. The other team, the Hoppers, had 44 points. Nick's best friend, Reid, was playing in the game too. They had practiced a play they called "Switchfoot" all week. They called it that because they pretended to run one way with the basketball and then switched direction. They hoped to fool the other team.

This was their chance. With 10 seconds left in the game, Reid had the ball. A player on the Hoppers almost grabbed the ball away. "Switchfoot!" yelled Reid. Nick changed direction. Reid passed the ball to him. The clock ticked down . . . three seconds . . . two seconds . . . .

With one second left, Nick raised the ball, jumped up, threw it at the hoop, and BUZZZZ!

"Whaaaat?" asked Nick as he rubbed his eyes. He reached over to turn off the alarm on his clock.

"Get up or you're going to be late for school," said Mom. "And don't forget to feed Switchfoot. He's still a puppy and needs his breakfast!" Nick looked at his puppy and smiled.

## Before Reading

- Do you like to play or watch sports?
- Have you ever been on any kind of team?

## During Reading

- Which team is in the lead?
- Why is the play called "Switchfoot"?

## After Reading

- Did the Eagles win the basketball championship game?
- Who is Switchfoot?

## Vocabulary

buzzer: an alarm on a clock

pass: to throw a ball from one person to another

hoop: a round metal rim with a hanging net used for basketball

# Identify Cause and Effect

**Cause** tells why something happened. The **effect** is what happens as a result of something. Some things in "The Buzzer" tell about what happened in a dream that Nick had. Some of the things we learn in the story help explain why Nick may have had a dream about basketball. Draw a line connecting the causes and effects below:

## Effects

1. Nick's dream was about basketball.

2. He made a shot at the buzzer.

3. The secret play was named Switchfoot.

## Causes

A. Nick's alarm clock buzzer went off.

B. Nick played basketball right before he went to bed.

C. Nick's dog was named Switchfoot.

Draw a scene from Nick's dream.

# Visualize

Do you have dreams when you sleep? Is there something you've always wanted to do? Draw a picture of your dream. Write a short description of your dream.

Could your dream come true? Is it something that could really happen? What would you need to do to make your dream come true?

To make my dream come true, _____

_____

_____

_____

_____

_____

# Comprehension Practice

Circle the letter of the best answer.

1. What did Nick and Reid do together?
   A. practice basketball
   B. read sports magazines
   C. draw their dreams
   D. play with Nick's puppy

2. Who is Switchfoot?
   A. Reid's fish
   B. Nick's basketball coach
   C. Reid's little brother
   D. Nick's puppy

3. What was really making the buzzing sound?
   A. bees outside
   B. the alarm clock
   C. the smoke detector
   D. the television

4. Someday, Nick will probably want to _____.
   A. play in a basketball championship
   B. take care of puppies
   C. be a coach
   D. be called Switchfoot

5. What is Nick's favorite activity?
   A. chasing his puppy
   B. playing basketball
   C. telling Reid what to do
   D. coaching basketball

6. In the second paragraph, what does **switched** mean?
   A. faked
   B. remained
   C. won
   D. changed

7. What caused Reid to yell "Switchfoot" during the game?
   A. They needed a shot to win the game.
   B. The other team had already won.
   C. Reid saw Switchfoot in the audience.
   D. Switchfoot is Reid's nickname for Nick.

8. How do you imagine Nick's room based on the story?
   A. His room is full of his puppy's toys.
   B. He has a basketball by his bed.
   C. There are posters of baseball players on the walls.
   D. His closet is full of hockey equipment.

# This Is the Way We Fly a Kite

Suzy looked out the window. She said, "It is sunny. It is warm. There is a breeze. It is a perfect day to fly a kite!"

## Before Reading

- Where could you fly a kite?
- Did you ever show or tell someone how to do something?

## During Reading

- Where do they go to fly the kite?
- Why do they need to go there to fly the kite?

## After Reading

- What kind of day is good to fly a kite?
- Was Suzy a good teacher? Why or why not?

## Vocabulary

kite: a flying toy that climbs in a breeze at the end of a long string

breeze: a gentle wind

cheer: to shout with happiness

Suzy called to her brother Mark, "Get your shoes on. Today you will learn to fly a kite!"

Suzy went to the garage and got her kite. It was red and white. "We need room to run. We will go to the park," Suzy said to Mark.

"Yippee! I love to run!" shouted Mark.

Suzy told Mark, "I will tell you what to do. First, hold the kite up. The end with the string faces down. Next, hold

the bottom of the kite in one hand. Hold the string with your other hand. Last, run! Let go of the kite and keep holding the string."

They both gave it a try. "Run, run, run!" yelled Mark. "Up, up, up it goes!"

"Now it is in the sky," said Suzy. "Now we hold the string and let it fly high! When it is time to go, we will pull the kite down."

"I love flying a kite," said Mark.

"I love flying a kite too," said Suzy.

"This is the way we fly a kite!" they both cheered.

# Identify Story Elements

Read "This Is the Way We Fly a Kite." Answer the questions to tell about the characters, setting, and plot of the story.

**Characters**

How many characters are in the story?

_____

What are the characters' names?

_____

How do they know each other?

_____


**Setting**

What season might it be?

_____

Where do the characters go in the story?

_____


**Plot**

What happens in the beginning of the story?

_____

What happens in the middle of the story?

_____

What happens at the end of the story?

_____

# Identify Sequence

Pay attention to the details as you read "This Is the Way We Fly a Kite." Think about what Suzy tells Mark. Tell in your own words the directions that Suzy gives to Mark to fly the kite.

**Step 1:** _____

**Step 2:** _____

**Step 3:** _____

**Draw a picture of Suzy and Mark flying the kite at the end.**

# Comprehension Practice

Circle the letter of the best answer.

1. What was the weather like?
   A. rainy
   B. snowy
   C. sunny
   D. foggy

2. Where did Suzy get the kite?
   A. from the garage
   B. at the park
   C. from a closet
   D. at the store

3. What helps a kite to fly?
   A. the motor
   B. electricity
   C. the wind
   D. the sun

4. What happened at the end of the story?
   A. Suzy got in trouble.
   B. Suzy and Mark cheered.
   C. Mark got lost.
   D. Suzy and Mark found money.

5. What is another title for this story?
   A. How to Fly a Kite
   B. A Sunny Day in Paris
   C. The Kite Movie
   D. The First Kite Ever Made

6. Suzy tells Mark "We need room to run." What does **room** mean in this sentence?
   A. wind
   B. a bedroom
   C. a rope
   D. space

7. Where do Suzy and Mark fly their kite?
   A. in their room
   B. at the park
   C. at school
   D. in their backyard

8. What is the first thing to do to fly a kite?
   A. run fast
   B. let the string go
   C. get on the kite
   D. hold the kite up

 #50087 Reading Comprehension—Level B

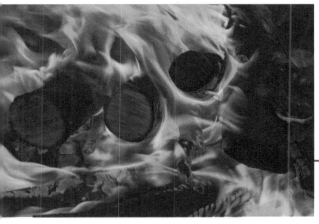

# A Camping You Can Go

## Before Reading

- What activities do you like to do?
- Have you ever gone to camp?

## During Reading

- What things do you do at a sports camp?
- What different activities could you do at an art camp?

## After Reading

- What is a day camp?
- What kinds of camps are there?

## Vocabulary

camp: a place where people come together to share common interests and activities

instrument: something that makes music

interest: a curiosity about something

There are many different types of camps. There are sports camps, animal camps, art camps, and school camps. Camps can meet after school, on weekends, or during school breaks.

Some camps are all about sports. At a sports camp, you may learn sports skills or play sports games. The sports might be soccer, baseball, basketball, tennis, or other sports.

Some camps have to do with music and art. Here you may play an instrument, sing, or even dance! You can also sketch, paint, sculpt, or weave.

Other camps have activities like those you do in school. You might write stories and poetry, read books, practice math skills, and even do science experiments.

A day camp is a camp where you go for part of a day. Someone takes you there and picks you up. You might even ride on a bus.

A sleepover camp is where you spend the night. You might stay for a night or two, or even a week or more. You might even sit around a campfire at night roasting marshmallows and telling scary stories!

There are camps for just about every interest you have. What kind of camp would you like to go to?

# Ask Questions

As you read, you might have questions about the topic or details. Asking questions as you read can help you understand better. You may find you are interested in the topic and want to make notes of questions you want to answer later.

In "A Camping You Can Go," you read about different kinds of camps. Did you have questions about what you read? Below are four different topics that you read about. Write any questions you might have about each topic.

| Topics | Questions |
|---|---|
| **1.** Types of camps | |
| **2.** Meeting times of camps | |
| **3.** Length of camps | |
| **4.** People at camps | |

# Use Prior Knowledge and Make Connections

Write "Yes" or "No" to tell whether you knew these facts before you read the story "A Camping You Can Go." If you wrote "Yes," then tell details about what you knew. This will help you see what you already knew about camps and what you learned about the topic.

| Facts in the Story | Did You Know This Fact? |
|---|---|
| 1. There are many different types of camps. | |
| 2. Camps can meet after school, on weekends, or during school breaks. | |
| 3. You learn and practice skills at a sports camp. | |
| 4. Some camps have activities like you do in school. | |
| 5. Some camps are sleepover camps. | |

Write about two other things you already knew about camps.

_____

_____

_____

_____

# Comprehension Practice

Circle the letter of the best answer.

1. Which type of camp is not listed in the story?
   A. soccer camp
   B. art camp
   C. cooking camp
   D. music camp

2. What kinds of things can you do at an art camp?
   A. sketch, paint, sculpt, or weave
   B. punt, kick, pass, tackle
   C. read, sleep, tell scary stories
   D. count, cook, read, kick

3. If you don't like being away from home overnight, which camp would you NOT like?
   A. day camp
   B. after school camp
   C. sleepover camp
   D. boot camp

4. According to the author, there are camps for _____.
   A. dogs and cats
   B. just about every interest you have
   C. parents
   D. your teacher

5. What is the main idea of this story?
   A. Camps are only held during summers.
   B. There are many different types of camps.
   C. Sports camps are only for professional athletes.
   D. Boys and girls should not go to the same camps.

6. When you are **roasting** marshmallows, what are you doing?
   A. cooking them
   B. eating them
   C. making them
   D. telling them

7. Which of the following is the most logical question to ask about camping?
   A. How long do we sleep at a day camp?
   B. Do they teach multiplication at an arts camp?
   C. Do you have to be an animal to go to an animal camp?
   D. Can I learn to skate at a sports camp?

8. What would you need at a sleepover camp?
   A. a calculator
   B. paint brushes
   C. a tennis racket
   D. your pajamas

# Comprehension Review:
# Vocabulary—Word Meaning

Read each sentence. Use the information in the sentence to choose the meaning for the underlined word. Mark the answer.

1. My brother tripped and <u>injured</u> his leg.
   - **A.** inspected
   - **B.** saw
   - **C.** hurt
   - **D.** split

2. Mom will <u>prepare</u> dinner tonight.
   - **A.** make
   - **B.** see
   - **C.** eat
   - **D.** clean

3. The ice felt <u>frigid</u>.
   - **A.** slippery
   - **B.** cold
   - **C.** clear
   - **D.** warm

4. The teacher helped to settle the <u>dispute</u>.
   - **A.** grade
   - **B.** lunch
   - **C.** fight
   - **D.** joke

5. The sandpaper felt <u>coarse</u>.
   - **A.** rough
   - **B.** brown
   - **C.** prickly
   - **D.** smooth

# Comprehension Review:
## Vocabulary—Opposites

Read each sentence. Choose the word that means the **opposite** of the underlined word. Mark the answer.

1. The water bucket was <u>full</u>.
   A. clear
   B. dripping
   C. wet
   D. empty

2. Kristen was the <u>slowest</u> runner in the group.
   A. fastest
   B. nicest
   C. coldest
   D. shortest

3. The coach began the race by yelling "<u>Go</u>!"
   A. Stop!
   B. Come!
   C. Watch!
   D. Run!

4. The light was very <u>bright</u>.
   A. shiny
   B. yellow
   C. hot
   D. dull

5. The bed was very <u>firm</u>.
   A. light
   B. soft
   C. flat
   D. hard

# Comprehension Review:
# Vocabulary—Content Clues

Read each sentence. Use the information in the sentence to choose the best word to complete the sentence. Mark the answer.

1. The _____ drove down the highway.
   A. bike
   B. dog
   C. car
   D. train

2. I learned how to tie my _____ when I was five years old.
   A. shoes
   B. pillow
   C. shirt
   D. bow

3. I _____ because I was tired.
   A. sneezed
   B. laughed
   C. yelled
   D. yawned

4. The ball _____ into the street.
   A. ran
   B. tipped
   C. rolled
   D. rushed

5. The _____ flew in the air.
   A. plane
   B. dog
   C. rope
   D. truck

# Comprehension Review: Sentence Completion

One word does not fit in each sentence. Use the sentence clues to choose that word. Mark the word that does NOT fit.

1. I love to play _____.
   A. baseball
   B. lamp
   C. checkers
   D. cards

2. The _____ jumped over the fence.
   A. horse
   B. plane
   C. dog
   D. cat

3. The park has many _____.
   A. swings
   B. slides
   C. books
   D. rides

4. We will eat _____ at the party.
   A. cake
   B. chips
   C. apples
   D. rocks

5. The _____ makes beautiful music.
   A. piano
   B. violin
   C. candle
   D. flute

# Comprehension Review:
# Main Idea

Read each story. Mark the sentence that tells the main idea.

1. The soccer game was cancelled because Mary was sick. It was also raining. The game will be tomorrow instead.

   A. Mary was sick.
   B. It was raining.
   C. The soccer game was cancelled.
   D. The game will be tomorrow.

2. I like to ski. I like to make snow angels. My favorite thing to do is make a snowman. There are many things I like to do in the snow.

   A. I like to make snow angels.
   B. There are many things I like to do in the snow.
   C. I like to ski.
   D. My favorite thing to do is make a snowman.

# Comprehension Review:
# Stated Details

Read the paragraph. Use the information in the paragraph to complete the sentences. Mark the answers.

Nick is in second grade. Nick loves to play basketball. He is on a team with nine of his friends. Their first game is Saturday. He hopes they will win!

1. Nick is a _____.
   - **A.** ball
   - **C.** boy
   - **B.** friend
   - **D.** team

2. Nick _____ basketball.
   - **A.** tries
   - **C.** hates
   - **B.** plays
   - **D.** dislikes

3. He plays with _____ friends.
   - **A.** nine
   - **C.** some
   - **B.** ten
   - **D.** young

4. The game is on _____.
   - **A.** Sunday
   - **C.** his birthday
   - **B.** the playground
   - **D.** Saturday

5. He _____ they will win.
   - **A.** thinks
   - **C.** dreams
   - **B.** hopes
   - **D.** says

# Comprehension Review:
# Classify/Categorize

Read each group of words. Mark the word that does NOT fit in the same category as the other words.

1. **A.** cookie
   **B.** cake
   **C.** flower
   **D.** pie

2. **A.** car
   **B.** bike
   **C.** bus
   **D.** driver

3. **A.** toe
   **B.** hat
   **C.** arm
   **D.** ear

4. **A.** yellow
   **B.** green
   **C.** swing
   **D.** red

5. **A.** book
   **B.** shirt
   **C.** jeans
   **D.** coat

# Comprehension Review: Sequence

Read the set of sentences. The sentences tell something that happened, but the sentences are not in the correct order. Choose the sentence that tells what happened last in each set.

1. **A.** It started raining.
   **B.** We put our wet clothes in the dryer.
   **C.** The sky got dark.
   **D.** We ran inside.

2. **A.** I ate the sandwich.
   **B.** I put the ham on the bread.
   **C.** I put the bread on the plate.
   **D.** I took out the bread, ham, and plate.

3. **A.** There was a nail in the road.
   **B.** We pulled the car to the side of the road.
   **C.** The tire was flat.
   **D.** Dad changed the tire.

4. **A.** We sang songs around the campfire.
   **B.** We gathered wood.
   **C.** We went camping.
   **D.** "Let's make a fire," I said.

5. **A.** My hair was in my face.
   **B.** I went to the barber.
   **C.** "Nice haircut," Mom said.
   **D.** Mom made an appointment.

# Comprehension Review:
# Plot, Setting, Characters

Read each selection. Use the information to answer the questions. Mark the answers.

Amy moved to a new home. Amy's mom, dad, and Amy unloaded the truck. Amy unpacked her things.

1. Where does the story take place?
   A. the moving truck
   B. their old home
   C. their new home
   D. the kitchen

2. Who are the characters in the story?
   A. dad and the truck
   B. mom and the moving men
   C. the new and old home
   D. Amy, Mom, and Dad

It was Mike's birthday. He was having a party at his home. Ten friends came with presents. He was very excited.

3. Where does the story take place?
   A. Mike's house
   B. Mike's presents
   C. Mike's friends
   D. Mike's birthday

4. What happens in the story?
   A. Mike is having a bad day.
   B. There is a party at Mike's house.
   C. The presents are wrapped.
   D. Mike plays with his friends.

# Comprehension Review:
# Predict

Read each paragraph. Use the information to predict what will happen. Mark the answers.

1. Sam leaned back on his chair. "Don't tip your chair," said mom. Sam's chair slipped.
   What will happen next?
   A. Sam will fall.
   B. Sam will eat.
   C. Sam will tip.
   D. Sam will stand.

2. It was test time. Mary's pencil lead broke. Mary went to the pencil sharpener.
   What will Mary do next?
   A. get a new pencil
   B. take the test
   C. sharpen her pencil
   D. read a book

3. The phone rang. Mom was busy. Dad walked to the phone. What will happen next?
   A. Mom will answer the phone.
   B. They will eat dinner.
   C. The doorbell will ring.
   D. Dad will answer the phone.

 #50087 Reading Comprehension—Level B

# Comprehension Review:
# Make Inferences

Read the sentences. Use the information in the sentence to guess the item. Mark the answer.

1. It is green.
   It grows on the ground.
   We sit on it for picnics.
   It is _____.
   A. a tree
   B. flowers
   C. grass
   D. a blanket

2. You read it.
   You can buy it.
   You can borrow it from a library.
   It is a _____.
   A. book
   B. radio
   C. movie
   D. game

3. I help when it is cold.
   You can snuggle with me.
   I am on a bed.
   I am a _____.
   A. heater
   B. candle
   C. blanket
   D. rug

# Comprehension Review:
# Cause and Effect

Read each sentence. Mark the cause or effect for the sentence.

1. Dan lost his coat and it was cold outside.
   A. Dan runs.
   B. Dan jumps.
   C. Dan gets a cold.
   D. Dan catches a fish.

2. Sara laughed because _____
   A. she got a bad grade.
   B. someone tickled her.
   C. she was sad.
   D. she was hungry.

3. The little girl was afraid of water.
   A. She will swim in the lake.
   B. She will swim in the pool.
   C. She will not go swimming.
   D. She will jump off of the diving board.

4. The mailman delivered ten cards to my house.
   A. It is my birthday.
   B. I am going on a trip.
   C. It is my teacher's birthday.
   D. I am hungry.

5. My brother has a sore leg.
   A. He has homework.
   B. He is in trouble.
   C. He loves to read.
   D. He fell on the ice.

#50087 Reading Comprehension—Level B